Texts and Monographs in Computer Science

PROGRAMMING IN MODULA-2

Niklaus Wirth

Second, Corrected Edition

Springer-Verlag
Berlin Heidelberg New York 1983

Professor Dr. Niklaus Wirth
Institut für Informatik, ETH, CH-8092 Zürich

Professor David Gries
Department of Computer Science, Cornell University
Ithaca, NY 14853, USA

The 1st edition was published as a monograph,
ISBN 3-540-11674-5
Springer-Verlag Berlin Heidelberg New York 1982

ISBN 3-540-12206-0 Springer-Verlag Berlin Heidelberg New York
ISBN 0-387-12206-0 Springer-Verlag New York Heidelberg Berlin

Library of Congress Cataloging in Publication Data
Wirth, Niklaus.
Programming in Modula-2.
Bibliography: p.
Includes index.
1. Modula-2 (Computer program language) I. Title.
QA76.73.M63W5713   1983   001.64'24   83-434
ISBN 0-387-12206-0 (New York)

Printing: Beltz, Hemsbach. Bookbinding: Schäffer, Grünstadt
2145/3140-543210

Contents

Preface

This text is an introduction to programming in general, and a manual for programming with the language Modula-2 in particular. It is oriented primarily towards people who have already acquired some basic knowledge of programming and would like to deepen their understanding in a more structured way. Nevertheless, an introductory chapter is included for the benefit of the beginner, displaying in a concise form some of the fundamental concepts of computers and their programming. The text is therefore also suitable as a self-contained tutorial. The notation used is Modula-2, which lends itself well for a structured approach and leads the student to a working style that has generally become known under the title of *structured programming*.

As a manual for programming in Modula-2, the text covers practically all facilities of that language. Part 1 covers the basic notions of the variable, expression, assignment, conditional and repetitive statement, and array data structure. Together with Part 2 which introduces the important concept of the procedure or subroutine, it contains essentially the material commonly discussed in introductory programming courses. Part 3 concerns data types and structures and constitutes the essence of an advanced course on programming. Part 4 introduces the notion of the module, a concept that is fundamental to the design of larger programmed systems and to programming as team work. The most commonly used utility programs for input and output are presented as examples of modules. And finally, Part 5 covers facilities for system programming, device handling, and multiprogramming. Practical hints on how and when to use particular facilities are included and are intended as guidelines for acquiring a sound style of programming and system structuring.

The language Modula-2 is a descendant of its direct ancestors Pascal [1] and Modula [2]. Whereas Pascal had been designed as a general purpose language and after implementation in 1970 has gained wide usage, Modula had emerged from experiments in multiprogramming and therefore concentrated on relevant aspects pertinent to that field of application. It had been defined and implemented experimentally by 1975.

In 1977, a research project with the goal to design a computer system (hardware **and** software) in an integrated approach, was launched at the Institut für Informatik of ETH Zürich. This system (later to be called Lilith) was to be programmed in a single high-level language, which therefore had to satisfy requirements of high-level system design as well as those of low-level programming of parts that closely interact with the given hardware. Modula-2 emerged from careful design deliberations as a language that includes all aspects of Pascal and extends them with the important module concept and those of multiprogramming. Since its syntax was more in line with that of Modula than with Pascal's, the chosen name was Modula-2. We shall subsequently use *Modula* as synonym for Modula-2.

The language's main additions with regard to Pascal are:

1. The *module* concept, and in particular the facility to split a module into a *definition part* and an *implementation part*.

2. A more systematic syntax which facilitates the learning process. In particular, every structure starting with a keyword also ends with a keyword, i.e. is properly bracketed.

3. The concept of the *process* as the key to multiprogramming facilities.

4. So-called *low-level facilities* which make it possible to breach the rigid type consistency rules and allow to map data with Modula-2 structure onto a store without inherent structure.

5. The *procedure type* which allows procedures to be dynamically assigned to variables.

A first implementation of Modula-2 became operational on the PDP-11 computer in 1979, and the language's definition was published as a Technical Report in March 1980. Since then the language has been in daily use in our institute. After a year's use and testing in applications, the compiler was released for outside users in March 1981. Interest in this compiler has grown rapidly, because it incorporates a powerful system design tool implemented on widely installed minicomputers. This interest had given rise to the need for this manual and tutorial. The defining report is included at the end of the manual, primarily for reference purposes. It has been left unchanged, with the exception that the chapters on standard utility modules and on the use of the compiler have been omitted.

This text has been produced in camera-ready form by a Lilith minicomputer connected to a Canon LBP-10 laser printer. Concurrently with the writing of the book, the author designed the programs necessary for automatic text formatting (and controlling the printer) and designed the interface connecting the printer. Naturally, all these programs have been written in Modula (for Lilith).

It is impossible to properly acknowledge all the influences that contributed to the writing of this text or the design of Modula. However, I am particularly grateful for the inspiring influence of a sabbatical year (1976) at the research laboratory of Xerox Corporation (PARC), and for the ideas concerning modules presented by the language Mesa [3]. Perhaps the most important insight gained was the feasibility of implementing a high-level language effectively on minicomputers. My thanks are also due to the implementors of Modula, notably L. Geissmann, A. Gorrengourt, Ch. Jacobi and S.E. Knudsen, who not only have turned Modula into an effective, reliable tool, but have often wisely consulted against the inclusion of further fancy facilities.

Zürich, February 1982   N. W.

References

1. N.Wirth. The programming language PASCAL.
   Acta Informatica 1, 35-63 (1971).

2. N.Wirth. Modula: a language for modular multiprogramming.
   Software - Practice and Experience, 7, 3-35 (1977).

3. J.G.Mitchell, W. Maybury, R.Sweet. Mesa Language Manual.
   Xerox PARC, CSL-78-1, (1978).

1. Introduction

Although this manual assumes that its reader is already familiar with the basic notions of computer and programming, it may be appropriate to start out with the explanation of some concepts and their terminology. We recognize that - with rare exceptions - programs are written - more appropriately: designed - with the purpose of being interpreted by a computer. The computer then performs a process, i.e. a sequence of actions, according to the specifications given by that program. The process is also called a computation.

The program itself is a *text*. Since it specifies a usually fairly complex process, and must do so with utmost precision and care for all details, the meaning of this text must be specified very precisely. Such precision requires an exact formalism. This formalism has become known as a *language*. We adopt this name, although a language is normally spoken and much less precisely defined. Our purpose here is to learn the formalism or language called **Modula-2** (henceforth simply called Modula).

A program usually specifies a process that causes its interpreter, i.e. the computer, to read data (the so-called *input*) from some sources and to vary its subsequent actions according to the accepted data. This implies that a program does not only specify a (single) process, but an entire - usually unbounded - class of computations. We have to ensure that these processes act according to the given specifications (or should we say expectations) in all cases of this class. Whereas we could verify that this specification is met in the case of a single computation, this is impossible in the general case, because the class of all permitted processes is much too large. The conscientious programmer ensures the correctness of his program by careful design and analysis. Careful design is the essence of professional programming.

The task of designing a program is further complicated by the fact that the program not only must describe an entire class of computations, but often should also be interpreted (executed) by different interpreters (computers). At earlier times, this required the manual transcription of the program from its source form into different computer codes, taking into account their various characteristics and limitations. The difficulties have been drastically reduced, albeit not eliminated, by the creation of high level languages with formal definitions and the construction of automatic translators converting the program into the codes of the various computers.

In principle, the formal language should be defined in an abstract, perhaps axiomatic fashion without reference to an actual computer or interpretation mechanism. If this were achieved, the programmer would have to understand the formal language only. However, such generality is costly and often restrictive, and in many cases the programmer should still know the principal characteristics of his computer(s). Nevertheless, the qualified programmer will make as little reference to specific computer characteristics as possible and rely exclusively on the rules of the formal language in order to keep his program general and portable. The language Modula assists in this task by confining computer dependencies to specific objects, used in so-called *low-level programming* only.

From the foregoing it follows that a translation process lies between the program's formulation and its interpretation. This process is called a *compilation,* because it condenses the program's source text into a cryptic computer code. The quality of this compilation may be crucial to the efficiency of the program's ultimate interpretation. We stress the fact that there may be many compilers for a given language (even for the same computer). Some may be more efficient than others. We recognize that efficiency is a characteristic of implementations rather than the language. It therefore is important to distinguish between the concepts of language and implementation.

We summarize:

A program is a piece of *text.*

The program specifies *computations* or processes.

A process is performed by an interpreter, usually a *computer,* interpreting (executing) the program.

The meaning of the program is specified by a formalism called *programming language.*

A program specifies a *class of computations,* the input data acting as parameter of each individual process.

Prior to its execution, a program text is translated into computer code by a *compiler.* This process is called a *compilation.*

Program design includes ensuring that all members of this class of computations act according to specification. This is done by careful *analytic verification* and by selective *empirical testing* of characteristic cases.

Programs should refrain from making reference to characteristics of specific interpreters (computers) whenever possible. Only the lack of such reference ensures that their meaning can be derived from rules of the language.

A *compiler* is a program translating programs from their source form to specific computer codes. Programs need to be compiled before they are executed. Programming in the wider sense not only includes the formulation of the program, but also the concrete preparation of the text, its compilation, correction of errors, so-called *debugging,* and the planning of tests. The modern programmer uses many tools for these tasks, including text editors, compilers, and debuggers. He also has to be familiar with the environment of these components. We shall not describe these aspects, but concentrate on the *language* Modula.

2. A first example

Let us follow the steps of development of a simple program and thereby explain some of the fundamental concepts of programming and of the basic facilities of Modula. The task shall be, given two natural numbers x and y, to compute their *greatest common divisor* (gcd).

The mathematical knowledge needed for this problem is the following:

1. if x equals y, x (or y) is the desired result

2. the gcd of two numbers remains unchanged, if we replace the larger number by the difference of the numbers, i.e. subtract the smaller number form the larger one.

Expressed in mathematical terms, these rules take the form

1. $gcd(x,x) = x$

2.   if $x > y$, $gcd(x,y) = gcd(x-y,y)$

The basic recipe, the so-called *algorithm*, is then the following: Change the numbers x and y according to rule 2 such that their difference decreases. Repeat this until they are equal. Rule 2 guarantees that the changes are such that gcd(x,y) always remains the same, and rule 1 guarantees that we finally find the result.

Now we must put these recommendations into terms of Modula. A first attempt leads to the following sketch. Note that the symbol # means "unequal".

```
WHILE x # y DO
  "apply rule 2, reducing the difference"
END
```

The sentence within quotes is plain English. The second version refines the first version by replacing the English by formal terms:

```
WHILE x # y DO
  IF x > y THEN
    x := x-y
  ELSE
    y := y-x
  END
END
```

This piece of text is not yet a complete program, but it shows already the essential characteristic of a *structured* programming language. Version 1 is a *statement*, and this statement contains another, subordinate statement (within quotes). In version 2 this is elaborated, and yet further subordinate statements emerge (expressing the replacement of a value x by another value x-y). This hierarchy of statements expresses the underlying structure of the algorithm. It becomes explicit due to the structure of the language, allowing the nesting of components of a program. It is therefore important to know the language's structure (syntax) in full detail. Textually we express nesting or subordination by appropriate indentation. Although this is not required by the rules of the language, it helps in the understanding of a text very considerably.

Reflecting an algorithm's inherent structure by the textual structure of the program is a key idea of structured programming. It is virtually impossible to recognise the meaning of a program when its structure is removed, such as done by a compiler when producing computer code. And we should keep in mind that a program is worthless, unless it exists in some form in which a human can understand it and gain confidence in its design.

We now proceed towards the goal of producing a complete program from the above fragment. We realize that we need to specify an action that assigns initial values to the variables x and y, as well as an action that makes the result visible. For this purpose we should actually know about a computer's facilities to communicate with its user. Since we do not wish to refer to a specific machinery, and particularly not in such a frequent and important case as the generation of output, we introduce *abstractions* of such communication facilites, postulating that they will be available - and realized in some appropriate fashion - on all computers where Modula programming is said to be possible. These abstractions take the form of standard statements, as shown below. The input of data is called a *Read* operation, their output as a *Write* operation. We may, for example, assume that data are read from a keyboard and written on a display.

```
ReadCard(x);
ReadCard(y);
WHILE x # y DO
  IF x > y THEN x : = x-y
      ELSE y : = y-x
  END
END;
WriteCard(x,6)
```

The procedure *ReadCard* reads a cardinal (a whole, non-negative number) and assigns it to its parameter (x). The procedure *WriteCard* outputs a cardinal as specified by its first parameter (x). The second parameter (6) indicates the number of digits available for the representation of this value on the output medium.

In the next and final version we complete our text such that it becomes a genuine Modula program.

```
MODULE gcd;
  FROM InOut IMPORT ReadCard, WriteString, WriteLn, WriteCard;

  VAR x,y: CARDINAL;
  BEGIN
  WriteString("x = "); ReadCard(x); WriteLn;
  WriteString("y = "); ReadCard(y); WriteLn;
  WHILE x # y DO
    IF x > y THEN x : = x-y
    ELSE y : = y-x
    END
  END;
  WriteString("gcd = "); WriteCard(x,6); WriteLn;
  END gcd.
```

The essential additions in this step are so-called *declarations.* In Modula, all names of objects occuring in a program, such as variables and constants, have to be declared. A declaration introduces the object's *identifier* (name), specifies the kind of the object (whether it is a variable, a constant, or something else) and indicates general, invariant properties, such as the type of a variable or the value of a constant.

The entire program is called a *module,* given a name (gcd), and has the following format:

```
MODULE name;
  <import lists>
  <declarations>
BEGIN
  <statements>
END name.
```

A few more comments concerning our example are in order. The procedures *WriteLn, WriteString, ReadCard,* and *WriteCard* are not part of the language Modula itself. They are defined in another module called *InOut* which is presumed to be available. A collection of such useful modules will be listed and explained in later parts of this text. Here we merely point out that they need to be imported in order to be known in a program. This is done by including the names of the needed objects in an import list and by specifying from which module they are requested.

The procedure *WriteString* outputs a *string,* i.e. a sequence of characters (enclosed in quotes). This output makes the computer user aware that an input is subsequently requested, an essential feature of conversational systems. The procedure *WriteLn* terminates a line in the output text.

And this concludes the discussion of our first example. It has been kept quite informal. This is admissible because the goal was to explain an existing program. However, programming is designing, creating new programs. For this purpose, only a precise, formal description of our tool is adequate. In the next chapter, we introduce a formalism for the precise description of correct, "legal" program texts. This formalism makes it possible to determine in a rigorous manner whether a written text meets the language's rules.

3. A notation to describe the syntax of Modula

A formal language is an infinite set of sequences of *symbols*. The members of this set are called sentences, and in the case of a programming language these sentences are *programs*. The symbols are taken from a finite set called the *vocabulary*. Since the set of programs is infinite, it cannot be enumerated, but is instead defined by rules for their composition. Sequences of symbols that are composed according to these rules are said to be syntactically correct programs; the set of rules is the *syntax* of the language.

Programs in a formal language then correspond to grammatically correct sentences of spoken languages. Every sentence has a structure and consists of distinct parts, such as subject, object, and predicate. Similarly, a program consists of parts, called syntactic entities, such as statements, expressions, or declarations. If a construct A consists of B followed by C, i.e. the concatenation BC, then we call B and C syntactic *factors* and describe A by the syntactic formula

$$A = BC.$$

If, on the other hand, an A consists of a B or, alternatively, of a C, we call B and C syntactic *terms* and express A as

$$A = B|C.$$

Parentheses may be used to group terms and factors. It is noteworthy that here A, B, and C denote syntactic entities of the formal language to be described, whereas the symbols =, |, parentheses, and the period are symbols of the meta-notation describing syntax. The latter are called *meta-symbols,* and the meta-notation introduced here is called *Extended Backus Naur-Formalism* (EBNF).

In addition to concatenation and choice, EBNF also allows to express option and repetition. If a construct A may be either a B or nothing (empty), this is expressed as

$$A = [B].$$

and if an A consists of the concatenation of any number of Bs (including none), this is denoted by

$$A = \{B\}.$$

This is all there is to EBNF! A few examples show how sets of sentences are defined by EBNF formulas:

(A|B)(C|D)	AC AD BC BD
A[B]C	ABC AC
A{BA}	A ABA ABABA ABABABA ...
{A|B}C	C AC BC AAC ABC BBC BAC ...

Evidently, EBNF is itself a formal language. If it suits its purpose, it must at least be able to describe itself! In the following definition of EBNF in EBNF, we use the following names for entities:

> statement: a syntactic equation
> expression: a list of alternative terms
> term: a concatenation of factors
> factor: a single syntactic entity or a parenthesized expression

The formal definition of EBNF is now given as follows:

> syntax   = {statement}.
> statement   = identifier "=" expression ".".
> expression   = term {"|" term}.
> term   = factor {factor}.
> factor   = identifier | string | "(" expression ")" |
>   "[" expression "]" | "{" expression "}".

Identifiers denote syntactic entities; strings are sequences of symbols taken from the defined language's vocabulary. For the denotation of identifiers we adopt the widely used conventions for programming languages, namely:

An identifier consists of a sequence of letters and digits, where the first character must be a letter. A string constists of any sequence of characters enclosed by quote marks (or apostrophes).

A formal statement of these rules in terms of EBNF is given in the subsequent chapter.

4. Representation of Modula programs

The preceding chapter has introduced a formalism, by which the structures of well-formed programs will subsequently be defined. It defines, however, merely the way in which programs are composed as sequences of symbols, in contrast to sequences of characters. This "shortcoming" is quite intentional: the representation of symbols (and thereby programs) in terms of characters is considered too much dependent on individual implementations for the general level of abstraction appropriate for a language definition. The creation of an intermediate level of representation by symbol sequences provides a useful decoupling between language and ultimate program representation. The latter depends on the available character set. As a consequence, we need to postulate a set of rules governing the representation of symbols as character sequences. The symbols of the Modula vocabulary are divided into the following classes:

identifiers, numbers, strings, operators and delimiters, and comments.

The rules governing their representation in terms of the standard ISO character set are the following:

1. *Identifiers* are sequences of letters and digits. The first character must be a letter.

$ identifier = letter {letter|digit}.

Examples of well-formed identifiers are

Alice   likely   jump   BlackBird   SR71

Examples of words which are no identifiers are

sound proof	(blank space is not allowed)
sound-proof	(neither is a hyphen)
2N	(first character must be a letter)
Miller's	(no apostrophe allowed)

Capital and lower-case letters are considered as distinct.

Sometimes an identifier has to be qualified by another identifier; this is expressed by prefixing i with j and a period (j.i); the combined identifier is called a *qualified identifier* (abbreviated as *qualident*). Its syntax is

$ qualident = {identifier "."} identifier.

2. *Numbers* are either integers or real numbers. The former are denoted by sequences of digits. Numbers must not include any spaces. Real numbers contain a decimal point and a fractional part. In addition, a scale factor may be appended. It is specified by the letter E and an integer which is possibly preceded by a sign. The E is pronounced as "times 10 to the power of".

Examples of well-formed numbers are

1981   1   3.25   5.1E3   4.0E-10

Examples of character sequences that are not recognized as numbers are

1,5	no comma may appear
1'000'000	neither may apostrophs
3.5En	no letters allowed (except the E)

The exact rules for forming numbers are given by the following syntax:

```
$   number = integer | real.
$   integer = digit {digit}.
$   real = digit {digit} "." {digit} [ScaleFactor].
$   ScaleFactor = "E" [" + "|"-"] digit {digit}.
```

Note: Integers are taken as octal numbers, if followed by the letter B, or as hexadecimal numbers if followed by the letter H.

3. *Strings* are sequences of any characters enclosed in quote marks. In order that the closing quote is recognized unambiguously, the string itself evidently cannot contain a quote mark. To allow strings with quote marks, a string may be enclosed within apostrophes instead of quote marks. In this case, however, the string must not contain apostrophes.

```
$   string = '"' {character} '"' | "'" {character} "'".
```

Examples of strings are

```
"no comment"
"Buck's Corner"
'he said "do not fret", and fired a shot'
```

4. *Operators and delimiters* are either special characters or *reserved words*. These latter are written in capital letters and must not be used as identifiers. Hence is it advantageous to memorize this short list of words.

The operators and delimiters composed of special characters are

+	addition, set union
-	subtraction, set difference
*	multiplication, set intersection
/	division, symmetric set difference
:=	assignment
&	logical AND
=	equal
# <>	unequal
<	less than
>	greater than
<=	less than or equal
>=	greater than or equal
( )	parentheses
[ ]	index brackets
{ }	set braces
(* *)	comment brackets
↑	dereferencing operator
, . ; : .. |	punctuation symbols

The reserved words are enumerated in the following list; their meaning will be explained throughout the subsequent chapters:

AND	ELSIF	LOOP	REPEAT
ARRAY	END	MOD	RETURN
BEGIN	EXIT	MODULE	SET
BY	EXPORT	NOT	THEN
CASE	FOR	OF	TO
CONST	FROM	OR	TYPE
DEFINITION	IF	POINTER	UNTIL
DIV	IMPLEMENTATION	PROCEDURE	VAR
DO	IMPORT	QUALIFIED	WHILE
ELSE	IN	RECORD	WITH

It is customary to separate consecutive symbols by a space , i.e. one or several blanks. However, this is mandatory only in those cases where the lack of such a space would merge the two symbols into one. For example, in "IF x = y THEN" spaces are necessary in front of x and after y, but could be omitted around the equal sign.

5. *Comments* may be inserted between any two symbols. They are arbitrary sequences of characters enclosed in the comment brackets (* and *). Comments are skipped by compilers and serve as additional information to the human reader. They may also serve to signal instructions (options) to the compiler.

5. Statements and expressions

The specification of an action is called a *statement*. Statements can be interpreted (executed), and that interpretation (execution) has an effect. The effect is a transformation of the state of the computation, the state being represented by the collective values of the program's variables. The most elementary action is the *assignment* of a value to a variable. The assignment statement has the form

$ assignment = designator ":=" expression.

and its corresponding action consists of three parts in this sequence:

1. evaluate the designator designating a variable,
2. evaluate the expression yielding a value,
3. replace the value of the variable identified in 1. by the value obtained in 2.

Simple examples of assignments are

$$i := 1$$
$$x := y + z$$

Here i obtains the value 1, and x the sum of y and z, and the previous values are lost. Observe that the following pairs of statements, executed in sequence, do not have the same effect:

$$i := i + 1; j := 2*i$$
$$j := 2*i; i := i + 1$$

Assuming the initial value $i = 0$, the first pair yields $i = 1, j = 2$, whereas the second pair yields $j = 0$. If we wish to exchange the values of variables i and j, the statement sequence

$$i := j; j := i$$

will not have the desired effect. We must introduce a temporary value holder, say k, and specify the three consecutive assignments

$$k := i; i := j; j := k$$

An *expression* is in general composed of several operands and operators. Its *evaluation* consists of applying the operators to the operands in a prescribed sequence, in general taking the operators from left to right. The operands may be constants, or variables, or functions. (The latter will be explained in a later chapter.) The identification of a variable will, in general, again require the evaluation of a designator. Here we shall confine our presentation to simple variables designated by an identifier. Arithmetic expressions (there exist other expressions too) involve numbers, numeric variables, and arithmetic operators. These include the basic operations of addition (+), subtraction (-), multiplication (*), and division. They will be discussed in detail in the chapter on basic data types. Here it may suffice to mention that the slash (/) is reserved for dividing real numbers, and that for integers we use the operator DIV which truncates the quotient.

An expression consists of consecutive *terms*. The expression

$$T0 + T1 + ... + Tn$$

is equivalent to

$$((T0 + T1) + ...) + Tn$$

and is syntactically defined by the rules

```
$   SimpleExpression = [" + "|"-"] term {AddOperator term}.
$   AddOperator = " + " | "-" | "OR".
```

Note: for the time being, the reader may consider the syntactic entities expression and SimpleExpression as equivalent. Their difference and the operators OR, AND, and NOT will be explained in the chapter on the data type BOOLEAN.

Each term similarly consists of *factors*. The term

$$F0 * F1 * ... * Fn$$

is equivalent to

$$((F0 * F1) * ...) * Fn$$

and is syntactically defined by the rules

```
$   term = factor {MulOperator factor}.
$   MulOperator = "*" | "/" | "DIV" | "MOD" | "AND" | "&".
```

Each factor is either a constant, a variable, a function, or an expression itself enclosed by parentheses.

Examples of (arithmetic) expressions are

```
2 * 3 + 4 * 5          = (2*3) + (4*5)  = 26
15 DIV 4 * 4           = (15 DIV 4)*4 = 12
15 DIV (4*4)           = 0
2 + 3 * 4 - 5          = 2 + (3*4)-5  = 9
6.25 / 1.25 + 1.5      = 5.0 + 1.5  = 6.5
```

The syntax of factors, implying that a factor may itself be an expression, is evidently recursive. The general form of designators will be explained later; here it suffices to know that an identifier denoting a variable or a constant is a designator.

```
$   factor = number | string | set | designator [ActualParameters] |
$        "(" expression ")" | "NOT" factor.
```

The rules governing expressions are actually quite simple, and complicated expressions are rarely used. Nevertheless, we must point out a few basic rules that are well worth remembering.

1. Every variable in an expression must previously have been assigned a value.

2. Two operators must never be written side by side. For instance a * -b is illegal and must be written as a*(-b).

3. The multiplication sign must never be omitted when a multiplication is required. For example, 2n is illegal and must be written as 2*n.

4. MulOperators are binding more strongly than AddOperators.

5. When in doubt about evaluation rules (i.e. precedence of operators), use additional parentheses to clarify. For example, a + b * c may just as well be written as a+(b*c).

The assignment is but one of the possible forms of statements. Other forms will be introduced in the following chapters. We enumerate these forms by the following syntactic definition

```
$   statement = [ assignment | ProcedureCall |
$           WhileStatement | RepeatStatement | ForStatement |
$           LoopStatement | IfStatement | CaseStatement |
$           WithStatement | ReturnStatement | "EXIT" ].
```

Several of these forms are structured statements, i.e. some of their components may be statements again. Hence, the definition of statement is, like that of expressions, recursive.

The most basic structure is the sequence. A computation is a sequence of actions, where each action is specified by a statement, and is executed after the preceding action is completed. This strict sequentiality in time is an essential assumption of sequential programming. If a statement S1 follows S0, then we indicate this sequentiality by a semicolon

$$S0; S1$$

This *statement separator* (not terminator) indicates that the action specified by S0 is to be followed immediately by the action corresponding to S1. A sequence of statements is syntactically defined as

```
$   StatementSequence = statement {";" statement}.
```

The syntax of statements implies that a statement may consist of no symbols at all. In this case, the statement is said to be empty and evidently denotes the null action. This curiosity among statements has a definite reason: it allows semicolons to be inserted at places where they are actually superfluous, such as at the end of a statement sequence.

6. Control Structures

It is a prime characteristic of computers that individual actions can be selected, repeated, or performed conditionally depending on some previously computed results. Hence the sequence of actions performed is not always identical with the sequence of their corresponding statements. The sequence of actions is determined by control structures indicating repetition, selection, or conditional execution of given statements.

6.1 Repetitive Statements

The most common situation is the repetition of a statement or statement sequence under control of a condition: the repetition continues as long as the condition is met. This is expressed by the while statement. Its syntax is

$ WhileStatement = "WHILE" expression "DO" StatementSequence "END".

and its corresponding action is

1. evaluate the condition which takes the form of an expression yielding the value TRUE or FALSE,

2. if the value is TRUE, execute the statement sequence and then repeat with step 1; if the value is FALSE, terminate.

The expression is of type BOOLEAN. This will be further discussed in the chapter on data types. Here it suffices to know that a simple comparison is a BOOLEAN expression. An example was given in the introductory example, where repetition terminates when the two comparands have become equal. Further examples involving while statements are:

1. Initially, let $q = 0$ and $r = x$; then count the number of times y can be subtracted from x, i.e. compute the quotient $q = x$ DIV y, and remainder $r = x$ MOD y, if x and y are natural numbers.

```
WHILE r >= y DO
  r := r-y; q := q + 1
END
```

2. Initially, let $z = 1$ and $i = k$; then multiply z k times by x, i.e. compute $z = x \uparrow k$, if z and k are natural numbers:

```
WHILE i > 0 DO
  z := z*x; i := i-1
END
```

When dealing with repetitions, it is important to remember the following points:

1. During each repetition, progress must be made towards meeting the goal, namely "getting closer" to satisfying the termination condition. An obvious corollary is that the condition must be somehow affected from within the repeated computation. The following statements are either incorrect or dependent on some critical precondition as stated.

```
WHILE i > 0 DO
    k := 2*k        (*i is not changed*)
END

WHILE i # 0 DO
    i := i-2        (*i must be even and positive*)
END

WHILE n # i DO
    n := n*i; i := i+1
END
```

2. If the condition is not satisfied initially, the statement is vacuous, i.e. no action is performed.

3. In order to obtain a grasp of the effect of the repetition, we need to establish a relationship that is stable, called an *invariant*. In the division example above, this is the equation $q*y + r = x$ holding each time the repetition is started. In the exponentiation example it is $z * x\uparrow i = x\uparrow k$ which, together with the termination condition $i = 0$ yields the desired result $z = x\uparrow k$.

4. The repetition of identical computations should be avoided (although a computer has infinite patience and will not complain). A simple rule is to avoid expressions within repetitive statements, in which no variable changes its value. For example, the statement

```
WHILE i < 3*N DO
    tab[i] := x + y*z + z*i; i := i+1
END
```

should be formulated more effectively as

```
n := 3*N; u := x + y*z;
WHILE i < n DO
    tab[i] := u + z*i; i := i+1
END
```

In addition to the while statement, there is the repeat statement, syntactically defined as

$ RepeatStatement = "REPEAT" StatementSequence "UNTIL" expression.

The essential difference to the while statement is that the termination condition is checked each time *after* (instead of before) execution of the statement sequence. As a result, the sequence is executed at least once. The advantage is that the condition may involve variables that are undefined when the repetition is started.

```
REPEAT
    i := i+5; j := j+7; k := i DIV j
UNTIL k > 23

REPEAT
    r := r-y; q := q+1
UNTIL r < y
```

The while and repeat statements are the most frequent and simple repetitive constructs. There exist others, notably the for statement, which will be introduced later when appropriate. The loop statement is a generalization of the repeat and while statements insofar as it permits the specification of terminating conditions at various points of the repeated statement sequence. Termination is simply indicated by the statement consisting of the single symbol EXIT. Although the LOOP statement is convenient in some cases, we recommend the use of the WHILE and REPEAT statements, because they more clearly exhibit a single condition of termination at a syntactically obvious point.

```
$   LoopStatement = "LOOP" StatementSequence "END".
```

6.2 Conditional Statements

The conditional statement, also called if statement, has the form

```
$   IfStatement =      "IF" expression "THEN" StatementSequence
$                      {"ELSIF" expression "THEN" StatementSequence}
$                      ["ELSE" StatementSequence]
$                      "END".
```

The following example illustrates its general form.

```
IF   R1 THEN S1
ELSIF R2 THEN S2
ELSIF R3 THEN S3
ELSE  S4
END
```

The meaning is obvious from the wording. However, it must be remembered that the expressions R1...R3 are evaluated one after the other, and that as soon as one yields the value TRUE, its corresponding statement sequence is executed, whereafter the IF statement is considered as completed. No further conditions are tested. Examples are:

```
IF x = 0 THEN s : = 0
ELSIF x < 0 THEN s : = -1
ELSE s : = 1
END

IF ODD(k) THEN z : = z∗x END

IF k > 10 THEN k : = k-10; d : = 1
ELSE d : = 0
END
```

The constructs discussed so far enable us to develop a few simple, complete programs as subsequently described. The first example is an extension of our introductory example computing the greatest common divisor gcd of two natural numbers x and y. The extension consists in the addition of two variables u and v, and statements which lead to the computation of the *least common multiple* (lcm) of x and y. The lcm and the gcd are related by the equation

$$lcm(x,y) * gcd(x,y) = x*y$$

```
MODULE gcdlcm;
   FROM InOut IMPORT ReadCard, WriteLn, WriteString, WriteCard;

   VAR x,y,u,v: CARDINAL;
```

```
      BEGIN
        WriteString("x = "); ReadCard(x); WriteLn;
        WriteString("y = "); ReadCard(y);
        u := x; v := y;
        WHILE x # y DO
          (*gcd(x,y) = gcd(x0,y0), x*v + y*u = 2*x0*y0*)
          IF x > y THEN
            x := x - y; u := u + v
          ELSE
            y := y - x; v := v + u
          END
        END ;
        WriteCard(x,6); WriteCard((u + v) DIV 2, 6); WriteLn
      END gcdlcm.
```

This example again shows the nesting of control structures. The repetition expressed by a while statement includes a conditional structure expressed by an if statement, which in turn includes two statement sequences, each consisting of two assignments. This hierarchical structure is made transparent by appropriate indentation of the "inner" parts.

Another example demonstrating a hierarchical structure computes the real number x raised to the *power* i, where i is a natural number.

```
      MODULE Power;
        FROM InOut IMPORT ReadCard, WriteString, WriteLn;
        FROM RealInOut IMPORT ReadReal, Done, WriteReal;

        VAR i: CARDINAL; x,z: REAL;
      BEGIN
        WriteString("x = "); ReadReal(x);
        WHILE Done DO
          WriteString(" ↑i = "); ReadCard(i);
          z := 1.0;
          WHILE i > 0 DO
            (* z * x↑i = x0↑i0 *)
            z := z*x; i := i-1
          END ;
          WriteReal(z,16); WriteLn;
          WriteString("x = "); ReadReal(x)
        END ;
        WriteLn
      END Power.
```

Here we subject the computation to yet another repetition: each time a result has been computed, another value pair x,i is requested. This outermost repetition is controlled by a Boolean variable *Done* which indicates whether a number x had actually been read. (This variable is imported and is given a value by the reading routine.)

The straight-forward computation of a power by repeated multiplication is, although obviously correct, not the most economical. We now present a more sophisticated and more efficient solution. It is based on the following consideration: The goal of the repetition is to reach the value i = 0. This is done by successively reducing i, while maintaining the invariant $z * x↑i = x0↑i0$, where x0 and i0 denote the initial values of x and i. A faster algorithm therefore must rely on decreasing i in larger steps. The solution given here halves i. But this is only possible, if i is even. Hence, if i is odd, it is first decremented by 1. Of course, each change of i must be accompanied by a corrective action on z in order to maintain the invariant. A detail: the subtraction of 1 from i is not expressed by an explicit statement, because it is performed implicitly by the subsequent division by 2. Two further details are noteworthy: The function ODD(i) is TRUE, if i is an odd number, FALSE otherwise. x and z denote real values, as opposed to integer values. Hence, they can represent fractions too.

```
MODULE Power;
  FROM InOut IMPORT ReadCard, WriteString, WriteLn;
  FROM RealInOut IMPORT ReadReal, Done, WriteReal;

  VAR i: CARDINAL; x,z: REAL;
BEGIN
  WriteString("x = "); ReadReal(x);
  WHILE Done DO
    WriteString(" ↑ i = "); ReadCard(i);
    z : = 1.0;
    WHILE i > 0 DO
      (* z * x↑i = x0↑i0 *)
      IF ODD(i) THEN z : = z*x END ;
      x : = x*x; i : = i DIV 2
    END ;
    WriteReal(z,16); WriteLn;
    WriteString("x = "); ReadReal(x)
  END ;
  WriteLn
END Power.
```

The next sample program has a structure that is almost identical to the preceding program. It computes the logarithm of a real number x whose value lies between 1 and 2. The invariant in conjunction with the termination condition (b = 0) implies the desired result sum = log2(x).

```
MODULE Log2;
  FROM InOut IMPORT WriteString, WriteLn;
  FROM RealInOut IMPORT ReadReal, Done, WriteReal;

  VAR x,a,b,sum: REAL;
BEGIN
  WriteString("x = "); ReadReal(x);
  WHILE Done DO
    (*1.0 <= x < 2.0*)
    WriteReal(x, 15);
    a : = x; b : = 1.0; sum : = 0.0;
    REPEAT
      (*log2(x) = sum + b*log2(a)*)
      a : = a*a; b : = 0.5*b;
      IF a >= 2.0 THEN
        sum : = sum + b; a : = 0.5*a
      END
```

```
        UNTIL b < 1.0E-7;
        WriteReal(sum,16); WriteLn;
        WriteString("x = "); ReadReal(x)
    END ;
    WriteLn
END Log2.
```

Normally, routines for computing standard mathematical functions need not be programmed in detail, because they are available from a collection of programs similar to those for input and output. Such a collection is, somewhat inappropriately, called a *program library*. In the following example, again exhibiting the use of a repetitive statement, we use routines for computing the cosine and the exponential function from a library called MathLib0 and generate a table of values for a damped oscillation. Typically, the available standard routines include the sin, cos, exp, ln (logarithm), sqrt (square root), and the arctan functions.

```
MODULE Oscillation;
 FROM InOut IMPORT ReadCard, WriteString, WriteLn;
 FROM RealInOut IMPORT ReadReal, WriteReal;
 FROM MathLib0 IMPORT exp, cos;

 CONST dx = 0.19634953;  (*pi/16*)
 VAR i,n: CARDINAL;
     x,y,r: REAL;
BEGIN
 WriteString(" n = "); ReadCard(n);
 WriteString(" r = "); ReadReal(r); WriteLn;
 i := 0; x := 0.0;
 REPEAT x := x + dx; i := i + 1;
  y := exp(-r*x) * cos(x);
  WriteReal(x, 15); WriteReal(y, 15); WriteLn
 UNTIL i >= n
END Oscillation.
```

7. Elementary data types

We have previously stated that all variables need be declared. This means that their names are introduced in the heading of the program. In addition to introducing the name (and thereby enabling a compiler to detect and indicate misspelled identifiers), declarations have the purpose of associating a *data type* with each variable. This data type represents information about the variable which is permanent in contrast, for example, to its value. This information may again aid in detecting inconsistencies in an erroneous program, inconsistencies that are detectable by mere inspection of the program text without requiring its interpretation.

The type of a variable determines its set of possible values and the operations which may be applied to it. Each variable has a single type that may be deduced from its declaration. Each operator requires operands of a specific type and produces a result of a specific type. It is therefore visible from the program text, whether or not a given operator is applicable to a given variable.

Data types may be declared in the program. Such constructed types are usually based on composition of basic types. There exist a number of most frequently used, elementary types that are basic to the language and need not be declared. They are called *standard types* and will be introduced in this chapter, although some have already appeared in previous examples.

In fact, not only variables have a type, but so do constants, functions, operands and (results of) operators. In the case of a constant, the type is usually deducible from the constant's notation, otherwise from its explicit declaration.

First we describe the standard data types of Modula, and thereafter elaborate on the form of declarations of variables and constants. Further kinds of data types and declarations are deferred to later chapters.

7.1 The type INTEGER

This type represents the whole numbers, and any value of type INTEGER is therefore an integer. Operators applicable to integers include the basic arithmetic operations

+	add
-	subtract
*	multiply
DIV	divide
MOD	remainder of division

Integer division is denoted by DIV and truncates the quotient. For example

```
 15 DIV 4   = 3
-15 DIV 4   = -3
 15 DIV (-4) = -3
```

The operator MOD produces the remainder of integer division such that, if we define

q = x DIV y, r = x MOD y ,

the equation

x = q•y + r, 0 <= r < y

is satisfied. x MOD y is defined for positive x and y only.

Sign inversion is denoted by the monadic minus sign. Furthermore, there exist the operators ABS(x) and ODD(x), the former yielding the absolute value of x, the latter the Boolean result "x is odd".

Every computer will restrict the set of values of type INTEGER to a finite set of integers, usually the interval $-2\uparrow(N-1) \ldots 2\uparrow(N-1)-1$, where N is a small integer, often 16 or 32, depending on the number of bits a computer uses to represent an integer. If an arithmetic operation produces a result that lies outside that interval, then *overflow* is said to have occured. The computer will give an appropriate indication and, usually, terminate the computation. The programmer should ensure that overflows will not result during execution of the program.

7.2 The type CARDINAL

Like INTEGER, the type CARDINAL represents whole numbers, but only non-negative values, i.e. the natural numbers and 0. The applicable operators are the same as for integers.

The advantage of using CARDINAL over INTEGER lies in making explicit the fact that a variable is positive valued only. We recommend the type CARDINAL for all cases where negative values do not (or should not!) occur..

The fact that negative values are strictly excluded from the set of cardinals requires care. A programmer used to the type INTEGER, for example, is likely to succumb to the following pitfall: Assume that a statement S is to be executed repeatedly with variable i having values N-1, N-2, ... , 1, 0. The statements

```
i := N-1;
WHILE i >= 0 DO
 S; i := i-1
END
```

will perform correctly, if i is of type INTEGER. However, if i is CARDINAL, the computation will fail, because it generates the value -1. The expression i >= 0 is, in fact, vacuous, because cardinals are always non-negative. The correct form of this piece of program is

```
i := N;
WHILE i > 0 DO
 i := i-1; S
END
```

A further advantage of the use of the type CARDINAL lies in the fact that a computer using N bits to represent a whole number will offer a range $0 \ldots 2\uparrow N-1$ for cardinals, whereas the largest value of type INTEGER is $2\uparrow(N-1)-1$. Moreover, multiplication and division is usually somewhat faster for operands of type CARDINAL.

Modula does not permit the use of operands of type INTEGER and CARDINAL in the same expression (so-called *mixed expressions*). The reason is that arithmetic instructions are different for the two types. The situation is somewhat eased by the presence of so-called *type transfer functions*. If i is of type INTEGER and c of CARDINAL, the expression i+c is disallowed, but i + INTEGER(c) is of type INTEGER, and CARDINAL(i) + c is of type CARDINAL.

7.3 The type REAL

Values of type REAL are real numbers. The available operators are again the basic arithmetic operations and ABS. Division is denoted by / (instead of DIV).

Constants of type REAL are characterized by having a decimal point and possibly a decimal *scale factor*. Examples of real number denotations are

$$1.5 \quad 1.50 \quad 1.5E2 \quad 2.34E\text{-}2 \quad 0.0$$

The scale factor consists of the capital letter E followed by an integer. It means that the preceding real number is to be multiplied by 10 raised to the scale factor. Hence

$$1.5E2 = 150.0, \quad 2.34E\text{-}2 = 0.0234$$

The important point to remember is that real values are internally represented as pairs consisting of a fractional number and a scale factor. This is called *floating-point representation*. Of course, both parts consist of a finite number of digits. As a consequence, the representation is inherently inexact, and computations involving real values are inexact because each operation may be subject to truncation or rounding.

The following program makes that inherent imprecision of computations involving operands of type REAL apparent. It computes the *harmonic function*

$$H(n) = 1 + 1/2 + 1/3 + ... + 1/n$$

in two different ways, namely once by summing terms from left to right, once from right to left. According to the rules of arithmetic, the two sums ought to be equal. However, if values are truncated (or even rounded), the sums will differ for sufficiently large n. The correct way is evidently to start with the small terms.

```
MODULE Harmonic;
  FROM InOut IMPORT ReadCard, Done, Write, WriteLn;
  FROM RealInOut IMPORT WriteReal;

  VAR i,n: CARDINAL;
     x,d,s1,s2: REAL;
  BEGIN
   Write("n = "); ReadCard(n);
   WHILE Done DO
     s1 : = 0.0; d : = 0.0; i : = 0;
     REPEAT
       d : = d + 1.0; i : = i+1;
        s1 : = s1 + 1.0/d;
     UNTIL i > = n;
     WriteReal(s1,16);
     s2 : = 0.0;
     REPEAT
```

```
          s2 := s2 + 1.0/d;
          d := d - 1.0; i := i-1
      UNTIL i = 0;
      WriteReal(s2,16); WriteLn;
      Write("n = "); ReadCard(n)
    END ;
    WriteLn
  END Harmonic.
```

The major reason for strictly distinguishing between real numbers and integers lies in the different representation used internally. Hence, also the arithmetic operations are implemented by instructions which are distinct for each type. Modula therefore disallows expressions with mixed operands.

However, integers can be transformed into real numbers (more exactly: internal representations as integers can be transformed into their corresponding floating-point representation) by explicit transfer functions, namely

$$\text{FLOAT(c)} \quad \text{TRUNC(x)}$$

FLOAT(c) is of type REAL and represents the value of the cardinal c; TRUNC(x) represents the truncated real value x and is of type CARDINAL. The programmer should be aware that different implementations of Modula may offer different or additional transfer functions.

7.4 The type BOOLEAN

A BOOLEAN value is one of the two logical *truth values* denoted by the standard identifiers TRUE and FALSE. Boolean variables are usually denoted by identifiers which are adjectives, the value TRUE implying the presence, FALSE the absence of the indicated property. A set of logical operators is provided which, together with BOOLEAN variables, form BOOLEAN expressions. These operators are AND (also denoted by &), OR, and NOT. Their results are explained as follows

```
p AND q  =  "both p and q are TRUE"
p OR q   =  "either p or q or both are TRUE"
NOT p    =  "p is FALSE"
```

The operators' exact definition, however, is slightly different, although the results are identical:

```
p AND q  =  IF p THEN q ELSE FALSE
p OR q   =  IF p THEN TRUE ELSE q
```

This definition implies that the second operand need not be evaluated, if the result is already known from the evaluation of the first operand. The notable property of this definition of Boolean connectives is that their result may be well-defined even in cases where the second operand is undefined. As a consequence, the order of the operands may be significant.

Sometimes it is possible to simplify Boolean expressions by application of simple transformation rules. A particularly useful rule is *de Morgan's law* stating the equivalences

```
(NOT p) AND (NOT q)  =  NOT (p OR q)
(NOT p) OR (NOT q)   =  NOT (p AND q)
```

Relations produce a result of type BOOLEAN, i.e. TRUE if the relation is satisfied, FALSE if not. For example

```
7  =  12     FALSE
7  <  12     TRUE
1.5 >= 1.6   FALSE
```

Such relations are syntactically classified as expressions, and the two comparands are so-called SimpleExpressions (see also chapter on expressions and statements). The result of a comparison is of type BOOLEAN and can be used in control structures such as if, while, and repeat statements. The symbols # and <> stand for unequal.

```
$  expression = SimpleExpression [relation SimpleExpression].
$  relation  = " = " | " # " | "<>" | "<" | "<=" | ">" | ">=" | "IN".
```

It should be noted that, similar to arithmetic operators, there exists a precedence hierarchy among the Boolean operators. NOT has the highest precedence, then follows AND (also called logical multiplication), then OR (logical addition), and last are the relations. As with arithmetic expressions, parentheses may be used freely to make the operators' association explicit. Examples of Boolean expressions are

```
    x  =  y
(x <= y) & (y < z)
(x > y) OR (y >= z)
  NOT p OR q
```

Note that a construct such as x < y & z < w is illegal.

Boolean values can be compared, and this not only for equality. Specifically,

```
FALSE < TRUE
```

Consequently, the logical implication "p implies q" is expressed either as

```
(NOT p) OR q    or as    p <= q.
```

The example above draws attention to the rule that the operands of an operator (including relational operators) must be of the same type. The following relations are therefore illegal

```
1  = TRUE
5  = 5.0
i+j = p OR q
```

Also incorrect is e.g. x <= y < z, which must be expanded into (x <= y) & (y < z). However, the following are correct Boolean expressions

```
i+j < k-m
p OR q = (i<j)
```

A final hint: although "p = TRUE" is legal, it is considered poor style and better expressed as p. Similarly, replace "p = FALSE" by "NOT p".

7.5 The type CHAR

Every computer system communicates with its environment via some input and output devices. They read, write, or print elements taken from a fixed set of characters. This set constitutes the value range of the type CHAR. Unfortunately, different brands of computers may use different character sets, which makes communication between them (i.e.

the exchange of programs and data) difficult and often tedious. However, there exists an internationally standardized set, the so-called ISO set.

The ISO standard defines a set of 128 characters, 33 of which are so-called *control characters*. The remaining 95 elements are visible printing characters shown in the following table. The set is ordered, and each character has a fixed position or *ordinal number*. For example, A is the 65th character and has the ordinal number 65. The ISO standard, however, leaves a few places open, and they can be filled with different characters according to national desires to establish national standards. Most widely used is the American standard, also called ASCII (American Standard Code for Information Interchange). Here we tabulate the ASCII set. The ordinal number of a character is obtained by taking its row number and adding its column number. These numbers are customarily given in octal form, and we follow this habit here too. The first two columns contain the control characters; they are customarily denoted by abbreviations hinting at their intended meaning. However, this meaning is not inherent in the character code, but only defined by its interpretation. At this point it suffices to remember that these characters are (usually) not printable.

	0	20	40	60	100	120	140	160
0	nul	dle		0	@	P	`	p
1	soh	dc1	!	1	A	Q	a	q
2	stx	dc2	"	2	B	R	b	r
3	etx	dc3	#	3	C	S	c	s
4	eot	dc4	$	4	D	T	d	t
5	enq	nak	%	5	E	U	e	u
6	ack	syn	&	6	F	V	f	v
7	bel	etb	'	7	G	W	g	w
10	bs	can	(	8	H	X	h	x
11	ht	em	)	9	I	Y	i	y
12	lf	sub	*	:	J	Z	j	z
13	vt	esc	+	;	K	[	k	{
14	ff	fs	,	<	L	\	l	|
15	cr	gs	-	=	M	]	m	}
16	so	rs	.	>	N	↑	n	~
17	si	us	/	?	O	←	o	del

Table of ASCII characters

Constants of type CHAR are denoted by the character enclosed in quote marks or in apostrophes. Character values can be assigned to variables of type CHAR, but these values cannot be used in arithmetic operations. Arithmetic operators can be applied, however, to their ordinal numbers obtained from the transfer function ORD(ch). Inversely the character with the ordinal number n is obtained with the transfer function CHR(n). These two complementary functions are related by the equations

$$CHR(ORD(ch)) = ch \quad and \quad ORD(CHR(n)) = n$$

for $0 <= n < 128$. They permit to compute the numeric value represented by the digit ch as

$$ORD(ch) - ORD("0")$$

and to compute the digit representing the numeric value n as

$$CHR(n + ORD("0"))$$

These two formulas depend on the adjacency of the 10 digits in the ISO character set, where ORD("0") = 60B = 48. They are typically used in routines converting sequences of digits into numbers and vice-versa. The following program piece reads digits and assigns the decimally represented number to a variable x.

```
x : = 0; Read(ch);
WHILE ("0" <= ch) & (ch <= "9") DO
    x : = 10*x + (ORD(ch) - ORD("0")); Read(ch)
END
```

Control characters are used for various purposes, mainly to control the functions of devices, but also to delineate and structure text. An important role of control characters is to specify the end of a line or of a page of text. There is no universally accepted standard for this purpose. We shall denote the control character signifying a line end by the identifier EOL (end of line); its actual value depends on the system used.

In order to be able to denote non-printable characters, Modula uses their octal ordinal number followed by the capital letter C. For example, 14C is a value of type CHAR denoting the control character ff (form feed) with ordinal number 14B.

7.6 The type BITSET

The values which belong to the type BITSET are sets of integers between 0 and N-1, where N is a constant defined by the computer system used. It is usually the computer's wordlength or a small multiple of it. Constants of this type are denoted as sets (see also chapter on set types). Examples are

$$\{5,7,11\} \quad \{0\} \quad \{8..15\} \quad \{0..3, 11, 15\} \quad \{\}$$

The notation m..n is a shorthand for m, m+1, ... , n-1, n.

```
$   set = [qualident] "{" [element {"," element}] "}".
$   element = ConstExpression [".." ConstExpression].
```

Operations on sets are:

+	set union
-	set difference
*	set intersection
/	symmetric set difference

Assuming that i denotes an element and u,v denote sets, these operations are defined in terms of set membership as

1. i IN (u+v) = (i IN u) OR (i IN v), i.e. the integer i is in the union u+v, if it is either in u or in v (or in both).

2. i IN (u-v) = (i IN u) AND NOT (i IN v), i.e. i is in the difference u-v, if it is in u, but not in v.

3. i IN (u*v) = (i In u) AND (i IN v), i.e. i is in the intersection u*v, if it is in both u and v.

4. i IN (u/v) = ((i IN u) # (i IN v)), i.e. i is in the symmetric difference u/v, if it is in either u or in v, but not in both.

The membership operator IN is regarded as a relational operator. The expression i IN u is of type BOOLEAN. It is TRUE, if i is a member of the set u. Bitsets are represented in computer systems as sets of bits, i.e. by the characteristic function of the set. The i'th bit of u, for example, is 1, if i is a member of u, 0 otherwise. Hence, the set operators are implemented as logical operations applied to the N members of the set variable. They are therefore very efficient and their execution time is usually even less than that of an addition of integers.

8. Constant and variable declarations

It has been mentioned previously that all identifiers used in a program must be declared in the program's heading, unless they are so-called standard identifiers known in every program (or are imported from some other module).

If an identifier is to denote a constant value, it must be introduced by a *constant declaration* which indicates the value for which the constant identifier stands. A constant declaration has the form

```
$  ConstantDeclaration  =  identifier " = " ConstExpression.
$  ConstExpression  =  SimpleConstExpression [relation SimpleConstExpression].
$  SimpleConstExpression  =  [" + "|"-"] ConstTerm {AddOperator ConstTerm}.
$  ConstTerm  =  ConstFactor {MulOperator ConstFactor}.
$  ConstFactor  =  qualident | number | string | set |
$            "(" ConstExpression ")" | "NOT" ConstFactor.
```

A ConstExpression is an expression containing constants only. Its syntax is analogous to that of expressions. A sequence of constant declarations is preceded by the symbol CONST. Example:

```
CONST   N = 16;
        EOL = 36C;
        empty = {};
        M = N-1;
```

Constants with explicit names aid in making a program readable, provided that the constants are given suggestive names. If, e.g., the identifier N is used instead of its value throughout a program, a change of that constant can be achieved by changing the program in a single place only, namely in the declaration of N. This avoids the common mistake that some instances of the constant, spread over the entire program text, remain undetected and therefore are not updated, leading to inconsistencies.

A *variable declaration* looks similar to a constant declaration. The place of the constant's value is taken by the variable's type which, in a sense, can be regarded as the variable's constant property. Instead of an equal sign, a colon is used.

```
$  VariableDeclaration = IdentList ":" type.
$  IdentList = identifier {"," identifier}.
```

Variables of the same type may be listed in the same declaration, and a sequence of declarations is preceded by the symbol VAR. Example:

```
VAR i,j,k: CARDINAL;
    x,y,z: REAL;
    ch: CHAR
```

9. The data structure Array

So far, we have given each variable an individual name. This is impractical, if many variables are necessary that are treated in the same way and are of the same type, such as, for example, if a table of data is to be constructed. In this case, we wish to give the entire set of data a name and to denote individual elements with an identifying number, a so-called *index*. The data type is then said to be structured - more precisely: array structured. In the following example, the variable a consists of N elements, each being of type CARDINAL, and the indices range from 0 to N-1.

```
VAR a: ARRAY [0..N-1] OF CARDINAL
```

An element is then designated by the array's identifier followed by its selecting index, e.g. a[i], where i is an expression whose value must lie within the index range specified in the array's declaration. Syntactically, a[i] is a *designator,* and the expression i is the *selector.* If, for example, all N elements of a are to be given the value 0, this can be expressed conveniently by a repetitive statement, where the index is given a new value each time.

```
i := 0;
REPEAT a[i] := 0; i := i + 1
UNTIL i = N
```

This example illustrates a situation that occurs so frequently that Modula provides a special control structure which expresses it more concisely. It is called the *for statement:*

```
FOR i := 0 TO N-1 DO
  a[i] := 0
END
```

Its general form is

```
$   ForStatement =
$   "FOR" identifier ":= " expression "TO" expression ["BY" ConstExpression] "DO"
$       StatementSequence
$   "END".
```

The expressions before and after the symbol TO define the range through which the so-called *control variable* (i) progresses. An optional parameter determines the incrementing (decrementing) value. If it is omitted, 1 is assumed as default value.

It is recommended that the for statement be used in simple cases only; in particular, no components of the expressions determining the range must be affected by the repeated statements, and, above all, the control variable itself must not be changed by the repeated statements. The value of the control variable must be considered as undefined after the for statement is terminated.

Some additional examples should demonstrate the use of array structures and the for statement. In the first one, the sum of the N elements of array a is to be computed:

```
sum : = 0;
FOR i : = 0 TO N-1 DO
   sum : = a[i] + sum
END
```

In the second example, the minimum value is to be found, and also its index. The repetition's invariant is $min = minimum(a[0], \dots, a[i-1])$.

```
min : = a[0]; k : = 0;
FOR i : = 1 TO N-1 DO
   IF a[i] < min THEN
      k : = i; min : = a[k]
   END
END
```

In the third example, we make use of the second to *sort* the array in ascending order:

```
FOR i : = 0 TO N-2 DO
   min : = a[i]; k : = i;
   FOR j : = i TO N-1 DO
      IF a[j] < min THEN
         k : = j; min : = a[k]
      END
   END;
   a[k] : = a[i]; a[i] : = min
END
```

Given the task to copy the values of array a to array b, we might be tempted to formulate this as

```
FOR i : = 0 TO N-1 DO
   b[i] : = a[i]
END
```

Although this is entirely correct, it is expressed more simply by the statement b := a; the assignment operator applies to entire arrays too.

The for statement is evidently appropriate, if *all* elements within a given index range are to be processed. It is inappropriate in most other cases. If, for example, we wish to find the index of an element equal to a given value x, we have no advance knowledge how many elements have to be inspected. Hence, the use of a while (or repeat) statement is recommended. This algorithm is known as *linear search.*

```
i : = 0;
WHILE (i < N) & (a[i] # x) DO
   i : = i + 1
END
```

From the negation of the continuation condition, applying de Morgan's law, we infer that upon termination of the while statement the condition $(i=N)$ OR $(a[i]=x)$ holds. If the latter term is TRUE, the desired element is found and i is its index; if $i = N$, no a[i] equals x.

We draw attention to the fact that the termination condition is a composite one, and that it is possible to simplify this condition by a common technique. Remember, that repetition must terminate, either if the desired element is found, or if the array's end is reached. The "trick" now consists in marking the end by a sentinel, namely the value x itself, which will automatically stop the search. All that is required is the addition of a dummy element a[N] at the array's end, serving as sentinel:

```
a: ARRAY [0..N] OF CARDINAL;

a[N] := x; i := 0;
WHILE a[i] # x DO i := i + 1 END
```

If upon termination i = N, no original element has the value x, otherwise i is the desired index.

A more challenging problem is the search for a desired element with value x in an array that is ordered, i.e. if a[i-1] <= a[i] for all i = 1 ... N-1. The best technique is the so-called *binary search:* inspect the middle element, then apply the same method to either the left or right half. This is expressed by the following piece of program, assuming N > 0. The repetition's invariant is

$$a[k] < x \quad \text{for all } k = 0 \ldots i\text{-}1 \quad \text{and} \quad a[k] > x \quad \text{for all } k = j+1 \ldots N\text{-}1$$

```
i := 0; j := N-1; found := FALSE;
REPEAT mid := (i + j) DIV 2;
  IF x < a[mid] THEN j := mid -1
  ELSIF x > a[mid] THEN i := mid + 1
  ELSE found := TRUE
UNTIL (i > j) OR found
```

Because each step halves the interval in which x is searched, the number of needed comparisons is only log2(N). A somewhat more efficient version which avoids the composite termination condition is

```
i := 0; j := N-1;
REPEAT mid := (i + j) DIV 2;
  IF x <= a[mid] THEN j := mid-1 END;
  IF x >= a[mid] THEN i := mid + 1 END
UNTIL i > j;
IF i > j + 1 THEN found ELSE not found END
```

An even more sophisticated version is given below. Its ingenious idea is not to terminate immediately when the element is found, which is rare compared to the number of unsuccessful comparisons.

```
i := 0; j := N-1;
REPEAT mid := (i + j) DIV 2;
  IF x < a[mid] THEN j := mid
  ELSE i := mid + 1
  END
UNTIL i >= j
```

This ends our list of examples of typical uses of simple arrays.

The elements of an array are all of the same type, but this type may again be an array (in fact, it may be any structure, as will be seen later). An array of arrays is called a *multidimensional array* or *matrix,* because each index may be considered as spanning a dimension in a Cartesian space. Examples of two-dimensional arrays are

```
a: ARRAY [1..N],[1..N] OF REAL
T: ARRAY [0..M-1],[0..N-1] OF CHAR
```

These are actually abbreviations of the following full forms

```
a: ARRAY [1..N] OF
    ARRAY [1..N] OF
      REAL

T: ARRAY [0..M-1] OF
    ARRAY [0..N-1] OF
      CHAR
```

where indentation is used to exhibit the hierarchical structure. The general syntax of an array type is

```
$   ArrayType = "ARRAY" SimpleType {"," SimpleType } "OF" type.
```

where the simple type denoting the index range either has the form

```
"[" ConstExpression ".." ConstExpression "]"
```

or is an identifier. For example, the array declaration

```
map: ARRAY CHAR OF CARDINAL
```

introduces an array of 128 cardinals where each element is indexed by a character value as shown by the statements

```
map["A"] : = 0; k : = map[" + "].
```

The syntax of designators allows for a similar abbreviation as used in declarations, namely a[i,j] in place of a[i][j]. The latter form expresses more clearly that [j] is the selector on the array a[i]. The syntax for the array element designator is

```
$   designator = qualident {"[" ExpList "]"}.
$   ExpList = expression {"," expression}.
```

In uses of matrices, the for statement comes to its full bloom, particularly in numeric applications. The canonical example is the multiplication of two matrices, where each element of the product $c = a*b$ is defined as

$$c[i,j] = a[i,1] * b[1,j] + a[i,2] * b[2,j] + ... + a[i,N] * b[N,j]$$

Given the declarations

```
a: ARRAY [1..M],[1..K] OF REAL;
b: ARRAY [1..K],[1..N] OF REAL;
c: ARRAY [1..M],[1..N] OF REAL
```

the multiplication algorithm consists of three nested repetitions as follows

```
FOR i : = 1 TO M DO
  FOR j : = 1 TO N DO
    sum : = 0.0;
    FOR k : = 1 TO K DO
      sum : = a[i,k]*b[k,j] + sum
    END;
    c[i,j] : = sum
```

```
    END
    END
```

In a second example we demonstrate the search of a word in a table, so-called *table search*, where each word is an array of characters. We assume the table is declared by the T given in the example above, and that x is given as

```
    x: ARRAY[0..N-1] OF CHAR
```

Our solution employs the typical linear search

```
    i : = 0; found : = FALSE;
    WHILE NOT found & (i < M) DO
       found : = "T[i] is equal to x";
       i : = i + 1
    END
```

If we define equality between two words x and y as $x[j] = y[j]$ for all $j = 0 ... N-1$, then the "inner" search can be expressed as

```
    j : = 0; equal : = TRUE;
    WHILE equal & (j < N) DO
       equal : = T[i,j] = x[j]; j : = j + 1
    END;
    found : = equal
```

This solution appears to be somewhat cumbersome. It is transformable into a simpler form, if M > 0 and N > 0. The complete table search is then expressible as

```
    i : = 0;
    REPEAT j : = 0;
       REPEAT B : = T[i,j] # x[j]; j : = j + 1
       UNTIL B OR (j = N);
       i : = i + 1
    UNTIL NOT B OR (i = M)
```

The result B means "the word x has not been found".

We have now laid enough ground work to develop meaningful, entire programs and shall present three examples, all of them involving arrays.

In the first example, the goal is to generate a list of *powers of 2*, each line showing the values 2↑i, i, and 2↑(-i). This task is quite simple, if the type REAL is used. The program then contains the core

```
    d : = 1; f : = 1.0;
    FOR exp : = 1 TO N DO
       d : = 2*d; write(d);  (* d = 2↑exp *)
       write(exp);
       f : = f/2.0; write(f) (* f = 2↑(-exp) *)
    END
```

However, our task shall be to generate exact results with as many digits as needed. For this reason, we present both the whole number $d = 2↑exp$ and the fraction $f = 2↑(-exp)$ by arrays of "digits", each in the range 0 ... 9. For f we require N , for d only log N digits. Note that the doubling of d proceeds from right to left, the halving of f from left to right. The table of results is shown below.

```
MODULE PowersOf2;
  FROM InOut IMPORT Write, WriteLn, WriteString, WriteCard;

  CONST M = 11; N = 32; (*M ~ N*log(2) *)
  VAR i,j,k,exp: CARDINAL;
    c,r,t: CARDINAL;
    d: ARRAY [0..M] OF CARDINAL;
    f: ARRAY [0..N] OF CARDINAL;
BEGIN
 d[0] : = 1; k : = 1;
 FOR exp : = 1 TO N DO
   (* compute d = 2↑exp by d : = 2*d *)
   c : = 0; (*carry*)
   FOR i : = 0 TO k-1 DO
     t : = 2*d[i] + c;
     IF t >= 10 THEN
       d[i] : = t - 10; c : = 1
     ELSE
       d[i] : = t; c : = 0
     END
   END ;
   IF c > 0 THEN
     d[k] : = 1; k : = k + 1
   END ;
   (*output d[k-1] ... d[0]*) i : = M;
   REPEAT i : = i-1; Write(" ") UNTIL i = k;
   REPEAT i : = i-1; Write(CHR(d[i] + ORD("0"))) UNTIL i = 0;
   WriteCard(exp, 4);
   (*compute and output f = 2↑(-exp) by f : = f DIV 2*)
   WriteString("  0."); r : = 0; (*remainder*)
   FOR j : = 1 TO exp-1 DO
     r : = 10*r + f[j]; f[j] : = r DIV 2;
     r : = r MOD 2; Write(CHR(f[j] + ORD("0")))
   END ;
   f[exp] : = 5; Write("5"); WriteLn
 END
END PowersOf2.
```

2	1	0.5
4	2	0.25
8	3	0.125
16	4	0.0625
32	5	0.03125
64	6	0.015625
128	7	0.0078125
256	8	0.00390625
512	9	0.001953125
1024	10	0.0009765625
2048	11	0.00048828125

4096	12	0.000244140625
8192	13	0.0001220703125
16384	14	0.00006103515625
32768	15	0.000030517578125
65536	16	0.0000152587890625
131072	17	0.00000762939453125
262144	18	0.000003814697265625
524288	19	0.0000019073486328125
1048576	20	0.00000095367431640625
2097152	21	0.000000476837158203125
4194304	22	0.0000002384185791015625
8388608	23	0.00000011920928955078125
16777216	24	0.000000059604644775390625
33554432	25	0.0000000298023223876953125
67108864	26	0.00000001490116119384765625
134217728	27	0.000000007450580596923828125
268435456	28	0.0000000037252902984619140625
536870912	29	0.00000000186264514923095703125
1073741824	30	0.000000000931322574615478515625
2147483648	31	0.0000000004656612873077392578125
4294967296	32	0.00000000023283064365386962890625

Our second example is similar in nature. Its task is to compute the *fractions* d = 1/i exactly. The difficulty lies, of course, in the representation of those fractions that are infinite sequences of digits, e.g. 1/3 = 0.333... . Fortunately, all fractions have a repeating period, and a reasonable and useful solution is to mark the beginning of the period and to terminate at its end. How do we find the beginning and the end of the period? Let us first consider the algorithm for computing the digits of the fraction.

Starting out with rem = 1, we repeat multiplying by 10 and dividing the product by i. The integer quotient is the next digit and the remainder is the new value of rem. This is precisely the conventional method of division, as illustrated by the following piece of program and the numeric example with i = 7:

```
1.000000 / 7 = 0.142857
1 0
  30
   20
    60
     40
      50
       1
```

```
rem := 1;
REPEAT rem := 10 * rem;
  nextDigit := rem DIV i;
  rem := rem MOD i
UNTIL ...
```

We know that the period has ended as soon as a remainder occurs which had been encountered previously. Hence, our recipe is to remember all remainders and their indices. The latter designate the place where the period had started. We denote these indices by x and give elements of x initial value 0. In the above explained division by 7, the values of x are

$$x[1] = 1, x[2] = 3, x[3] = 2, x[4] = 5, x[5] = 6, x[6] = 4$$

```
MODULE Fractions;
 FROM InOut IMPORT Write, WriteLn, WriteString, WriteCard;

 CONST Base = 10; N = 32;
 VAR i,j,m: CARDINAL;
   rem: CARDINAL;
   d: ARRAY [1..N] OF CARDINAL; (*digits*)
   x: ARRAY [0..N] OF CARDINAL; (*index*)
BEGIN
 FOR i := 2 TO N DO
  FOR j := 0 TO i-1 DO x[j] := 0 END ;
  m := 0; rem := 1;
  REPEAT m := m + 1; x[rem] := m;
   rem := Base * rem; d[m] := rem DIV i; rem := rem MOD i
  UNTIL x[rem] # 0;
  WriteCard(i,6); WriteString(" 0.");
  FOR j := 1 TO x[rem]-1 DO Write(CHR(d[j] + ORD("0"))) END ;
  Write("'");
  FOR j := x[rem] TO m DO Write(CHR(d[j] + ORD("0"))) END ;
  WriteLn
 END
END Fractions.
```

```
 2   0.5'0
 3   0.'3
 4   0.25'0
 5   0.2'0
 6   0.1'6
 7   0.'142857
 8   0.125'0
 9   0.'1
10   0.1'0
11   0.'09
12   0.08'3
13   0.'076923
14   0.0'714285
15   0.0'6
16   0.0625'0
17   0.'0588235294117647
18   0.0'5
19   0.'052631578947368421
20   0.05'0
21   0.'047619
```

```
26   0.0'384615
27   0.'037
28   0.03'571428
29   0.'03448275862068965517241379331
30   0.0'3
31   0.'032258064516129
32   0.03125'0
```

Our last example of a program computes a list of *prime numbers*. It is based on the idea of inspecting the divisibility of successive integers. The tested integers are obtained by incrementing alternatively by 2 and 4, thereby avoiding multiples of 2 and 3 ab initio. Divisibility needs to be tested for prime divisors only, which are obtained by storing previously computed results.

```
MODULE Primes;
 FROM InOut IMPORT WriteLn, WriteCard;

 CONST N = 500; M = 23;  (*M ~ sqrt(N)*)
   LL = 10; (*no. of primes placed on a line*)
 VAR i,k,x: CARDINAL;
   inc, lim, square, L: CARDINAL;
   prime: BOOLEAN;
   P,V: ARRAY [0..M] OF CARDINAL;
BEGIN L := 0;
 x := 1; inc := 4; lim := 1; square := 9;
 FOR i := 3 TO N DO
  (* find next prime number p[i] *)
  REPEAT x := x + inc; inc := 6 - inc;
   IF square <= x THEN
    lim := lim + 1; V[lim] := square;
    square := P[lim + 1] * P[lim + 1]
   END ;
   k := 2; prime := TRUE;
   WHILE prime & (k < lim) DO
    k := k + 1;
    IF V[k] < x THEN
     V[k] := V[k] + 2*P[k]
    END ;
    prime := x # V[k]
   END
  UNTIL prime;
  IF i <= M THEN P[i] := x END ;
  WriteCard(x,6); L := L + 1;
  IF L = LL THEN
   WriteLn; L := 0
  END
 END
END Primes.
```

```
 5     7    11    13    17    19    23    29    31    37
41    43    47    53    59    61    67    71    73    79
```

42

END
END Primes.

5	7	11	13	17	19	23	29	31	37
41	43	47	53	59	61	67	71	73	79
83	89	97	101	103	107	109	113	127	131
137	139	149	151	157	163	167	173	179	181
191	193	197	199	211	223	227	229	233	239
241	251	257	263	269	271	277	281	283	293
307	311	313	317	331	337	347	349	353	359
367	373	379	383	389	397	401	409	419	421
431	433	439	443	449	457	461	463	467	479
487	491	499	503	509	521	523	541	547	557
563	569	571	577	587	593	599	601	607	613
617	619	631	641	643	647	653	659	661	673
677	683	691	701	709	719	727	733	739	743
751	757	761	769	773	787	797	809	811	821
823	827	829	839	853	857	859	863	877	881
883	887	907	911	919	929	937	941	947	953
967	971	977	983	991	997	1009	1013	1019	1021
1031	1033	1039	1049	1051	1061	1063	1069	1087	1091
1093	1097	1103	1109	1117	1123	1129	1151	1153	1163
1171	1181	1187	1193	1201	1213	1217	1223	1229	1231
1237	1249	1259	1277	1279	1283	1289	1291	1297	1301
1303	1307	1319	1321	1327	1361	1367	1373	1381	1399
1409	1423	1427	1429	1433	1439	1447	1451	1453	1459
1471	1481	1483	1487	1489	1493	1499	1511	1523	1531
1543	1549	1553	1559	1567	1571	1579	1583	1597	1601
1607	1609	1613	1619	1621	1627	1637	1657	1663	1667
1669	1693	1697	1699	1709	1721	1723	1733	1741	1747
1753	1759	1777	1783	1787	1789	1801	1811	1823	1831
1847	1861	1867	1871	1873	1877	1879	1889	1901	1907
1913	1931	1933	1949	1951	1973	1979	1987	1993	1997
1999	2003	2011	2017	2027	2029	2039	2053	2063	2069
2081	2083	2087	2089	2099	2111	2113	2129	2131	2137
2141	2143	2153	2161	2179	2203	2207	2213	2221	2237
2239	2243	2251	2267	2269	2273	2281	2287	2293	2297
2309	2311	2333	2339	2341	2347	2351	2357	2371	2377
2381	2383	2389	2393	2399	2411	2417	2423	2437	2441
2447	2459	2467	2473	2477	2503	2521	2531	2539	2543
2549	2551	2557	2579	2591	2593	2609	2617	2621	2633
2647	2657	2659	2663	2671	2677	2683	2687	2689	2693
2699	2707	2711	2713	2719	2729	2731	2741	2749	2753
2767	2777	2789	2791	2797	2801	2803	2819	2833	2837
2843	2851	2857	2861	2879	2887	2897	2903	2909	2917
2927	2939	2953	2957	2963	2969	2971	2999	3001	3011
3019	3023	3037	3041	3049	3061	3067	3079	3083	3089
3109	3119	3121	3137	3163	3167	3169	3181	3187	3191

3203	3209	3217	3221	3229	3251	3253	3257	3259	3271
3299	3301	3307	3313	3319	3323	3329	3331	3343	3347
3359	3361	3371	3373	3389	3391	3407	3413	3433	3449
3457	3461	3463	3467	3469	3491	3499	3511	3517	3527
3529	3533	3539	3541	3547	3557	3559	3571		

Output of program Primes

These examples close the first part of this book. They show that arrays are a fundamental feature used in most programs. There exist hardly any programs of relevance outside the classroom which do not employ repetitions and arrays (or analogous data structures).

10. Procedures

Consider the task of processing a set of data consisting of a header and a sequence of N similar individual units. It might be generally described as

```
ReadHeader;
ProcessHeader;
WriteHeader;
FOR i : = 1 TO N DO
   ReadUnit; ProcessUnit;
   Write(i); WriteUnit
END
```

Clearly, the description of the original task has been made in terms of subtasks, emphasizing the dominant structure and supressing details. Of course, the subtasks *ReadHeader, ProcessHeader,* etc. must now be further described with all the necessary details. Instead of replacing these descriptive English words with elaborate Modula programs, we may consider these words as identifiers and define the details of the subtasks by textually separate pieces of program, called *procedures* (or subroutines). These definitions are called *procedure declarations,* because they define the actions of the procedure and give it a name. The identifiers in the main program referring to these declarations are said to be *procedure calls,* and their action is to invoke the procedure. Syntactically, the procedure call is a statement.

Procedures play a fundamental role in program design. They aid in displaying the algorithm's structure and in decomposing a program into logically coherent units. This is particularly important in the case of complex algorithms, i.e. of long programs. In the above example, it might be considered somewhat extravagant to declare separate procedures instead of merely substituting the refined program texts for the identifiers. Nevertheless, the gain in clarity of program structure often recommends the use of explicit procedures even in such a simple case. But of course procedures become particularly useful, if the same procedure is to be invoked at several points of the program.

A procedure declaration consists of the symbol PROCEDURE followed by the identifier (together they form the *procedure heading*), followed by the symbol BEGIN and the statements for which the procedure identifier stands and which are therefore called the *procedure body.* The declaration is terminated by the symbol END and the repetition of the identifier. The latter enables a compiler to detect mismatched endings of statements and declarations. The general syntax of procedure declarations will be given later. A simple example is the following, which computes the sum of a[0], ... ,a[N-1].

```
PROCEDURE Add;
BEGIN sum : = 0.0;
  FOR i : = 0 TO N-1 DO
    sum : = a[i] + sum
  END
END Add
```

The procedure concept becomes even much more useful due to two additional features that are coupled with it, namely the concepts of parameters and of locality of names. Parameters make it possible to invoke the same procedures at different points of the program applying the procedure to different values and variables as determined at the point of the call. Locality of names and objects is a concept considerably enhancing the procedure's role in structuring a program and compartmentalizing its parts. We shall first discuss the concept of locality.

Summarizing, we repeat the following essential points:

1. The procedure aids in exhibiting the inherent structure of a program and in decomposing a programming task.

2. If a procedure is called from two or more points, it reduces the length of the program and therefore the programming task and the potential for programming error. A further economic advantage is the reduction in the size of the compiled code.

11. The concept of locality

If we inspect the preceding example of procedure Add, we notice that the role of the variable i is strictly confined to the procedure body. This inherent locality should be expressed explicitly, and can be done by declaring i inside the procedure declaration. i thereby becomes a *local* variable.

```
PROCEDURE Add;
    VAR i: CARDINAL;
    BEGIN sum : = 0.0;
       FOR i : = 0 TO N-1 DO
          sum : = a[i] + sum
       END
    END Add
```

In some sense, the procedure declaration assumes the form of a separate program. In fact, any declaration possible in a program, such as constant-, type-, variable-, or procedure declaration, may also occur in a procedure declaration. This implies that procedure declarations may be nested and are defined recursively.

It is good programming practice to declare objects local, i.e. to confine the existence of an object to that procedure in which it has meaning. The procedure, i.e. the section of program text in which a name is declared, is called its *scope*. Since declarations can be nested, scopes are also nestable. The possibility of having objects local to some scope has several consequences. For example, the same name can be used to denote different objects. In fact, this is a most useful consequence, because a programmer is free to choose local identifiers without knowledge of those existing in the surrounding scope, as long as they do not denote objects used in the local scope (in which case he must obviously be aware of them anyhow). This decoupling of knowledge about different program parts is particularly useful and perhaps even vital in the case of large programs.

The rules of scope (validity of identifiers) are as follows:

1. The scope of an identifier is the procedure in which its declaration occurs, and all procedures enclosed by that procedure, subject to rule 2.

2. When an identifier i declared in a procedure P is redeclared in some inner procedure Q enclosed in P, then procedure Q and all procedures enclosed in Q are excluded from the scope of i declared in P.

3. The standard identifiers of Modula are considered to be declared in an imaginary procedure enclosing the program.

These rules may also be remembered by the algorithm in which the declaration of a given identifier i is searched: First, search the declarations of the procedure P in whose body i occurs; if the declaration of i is not among them, continue the search in the procedure surrounding P; then repeat this same rule until the declaration is encountered.

```
VAR a: CARDINAL;
PROCEDURE P;
```

```
      VAR b: CARDINAL;
      PROCEDURE Q;
         VAR b,c: BOOLEAN;
      BEGIN
         (*a, b(BOOLEAN), c are visible*)
      END Q;
   BEGIN
      (*a, b(CARDINAL) are visible*)
   END P
```

A consequence of the locality concept and of the rule that a variable does not exist outside its scope is that its value is lost when its declaring procedure is terminated. This implies that, when the same procedure is later called again, this value is unknown. The values of local variables are undefined when the procedure is (re)entered. Hence, if a variable must retain its value between two calls, it must be declared outside the procedure. The "lifetime" of a variable is the time during which its declaring procedure is active.

The use of local declarations has three significant advantages:

1. It makes clear that an object is confined to a procedure, usually a small part of the entire program.

2. It ensures that inadvertent use of a local object by other parts of the program is detected by the compiler.

3. It enables the implementation to minimize storage, because a variable's storage is released when the procedure to which the variable is local is terminated. This storage can then be reused for other variables.

12. Parameters

Procedures may be given *parameters*. They are the essential feature that make procedures so useful. Consider again the previous example of procedure Add. Very likely a program contains several arrays to which the procedure should be applicable. Redefining it for each such array would be cumbersome, inelegant, and can be avoided by introducing its operand as a parameter as follows.

```
PROCEDURE Add(VAR x: Vector);
  VAR i: CARDINAL;
BEGIN sum : = 0;
  FOR i : = 0 TO N-1 DO
    sum : = x[i] + sum
  END
END Add
```

The parameter x is introduced in the *parameter list* in the procedure heading. It thereby automatically becomes a local object, in fact is a place-holder for the actual array that is specified in the procedure calls

```
Add(a); ... ; Add(b)
```

The arrays a and b are called *actual parameters* which are substituted for x, which is called *formal parameter*. The formal parameter's specification must contain its type. This enables a compiler to check whether or not an appropriate actual parameter is supplied. We say that a and b, the actual parameters, must be compatible with the formal parameter x. In the example above, its type is Vector, presumably declared in Add's environment as

```
TYPE Vector = ARRAY [0..N-1] OF REAL;
VAR a,b: Vector
```

A better version of Add would include not only the array, but also the result sum as a parameter. We shall later return to this example. But first we need explain that there exist two kinds of formal parameters, namely *variable* and *value parameters*. The former are characterized by the symbol VAR, the latter by its absence.

We conclude this chapter by giving the syntax of procedure declarations and procedure calls:

```
$  ProcedureDeclaration = ProcedureHeading ";" block identifier.
$  ProcedureHeading = "PROCEDURE" identifier [FormalParameters].
$  block = {declaration} ["BEGIN" StatementSequence] "END".
$  FormalParameters = "(" [FPSection {";" FPSection}] ")" [":" qualident].
$  FPSection = ["VAR"] IdentList ":" FormalType.
$  FormalType = ["ARRAY" "OF"] qualident.

$  ProcedureCall = designator [ActualParameters].
$  ActualParameters = "(" [ExpList] ")".
```

Apart from the declaration of modules, we now have also encountered all forms of declarations.

```
$   declaration = "CONST" {ConstantDeclaration ";"} |
$           "TYPE"  {TypeDeclaration ";"} |
$           "VAR"   {VariableDeclaration ";"} |
$           ProcedureDeclaration ";" | ModuleDeclaration ";".
```

12.1 Variable parameters

As its name indicates, the actual parameter corresponding to a formal variable parameter (specified by the symbol VAR) must be a variable. The formal identifier then stands for that variable.

Example:

```
PROCEDURE exchange(VAR x,y: CARDINAL);
  VAR z: CARDINAL;
BEGIN z : = x; x : = y; y : = z
END exchange
```

The procedure calls

```
exchange(a,b); exchange(A[i], A[i + 1])
```

then have the effect of the above three assignments, each with appropriate substitutions made upon the call.

The following points should be remembered:

1. Variable parameters may serve to transmit a computed result outside the procedure.

2. The formal parameter acts as a place-holder for the substituted actual parameter.

3. The actual parameter cannot be an expression, and therefore not a constant either, even if no assignment to its formal correspondent is made.

4. If the actual parameter involves indices, these are evaluated when the formal-actual substitution is made.

5. The types of corresponding formal and actual parameters must be the same.

12.2 Value parameters

Value parameters serve to pass a value from the calling side into the procedure and constitute the predominant case of parameters. The corresponding actual parameter is an expression, of which a variable or a constant are a particular and simple case. The formal value parameter must be considered as a local variable of the indicated type. Upon call, the actual expression is evaluated and the result is assigned to that local variable. As a consequence, the formal parameter may later be assigned new values without affecting any part of the expression. In a sense, actual expression and formal parameter become decoupled as soon as the procedure is entered. As an illustration, we formulate the previously shown program to compute the power $z = x\uparrow i$ as a procedure.

```
PROCEDURE ComputePower(VAR z: REAL; x: REAL; i: CARDINAL);
BEGIN z : = 1.0;
  WHILE i > 0 DO
    IF ODD(i) THEN z : = z*x END;
    x : = x*x; i : = i DIV 2
```

```
        END
      END ComputePower
```

Possible calls are, for example

```
      ComputePower(u, 2.5, 3)
      ComputePower(A[i], B[i], 2)
```

Concerning value parameters, we must keep in mind that since the formal parameter represents a local variable, storage is needed for that variable. This may be of concern, if its type is an array of many elements. In this case, it is recommended to specify a variable parameter, even if this parameter is used for the import of values only.

Note that in the example above z and x are declared in distinct FP Sections, because "VAR z,x: REAL" would classify x as a variable parameter too, making it impossible to place a general expression in its corresponding actual parameter place.

12.3 Open array parameters

If a formal parameter type denotes an array structure, its corresponding actual parameter must be an array of the identical type. This implies that it must have elements of identical type and the same bounds of the index range. Often this restriction is rather severe, and more flexibility is highly desirable. It is provided by the facility of the so-called *open array* which requires that the types of the elements of the formal and actual arrays be the same, but leaves the index range of the formal array open. In this case, arrays of any size (number of elements) may be substituted as actual parameters. An open array is specified by the element type preceded by "ARRAY OF". For example, a procedure declared as

```
      PROCEDURE P(s: ARRAY OF CHAR)
```

allows calls with character arrays of arbitrary index bounds. The lower bound of the index range of the formal array is then always taken to be 0. The upper bound is obtained by calling the standard function HIGH(s). Its value is equal to the number of elements minus 1. Hence, if an array a declared as

```
      a: ARRAY[m..n] OF CHAR
```

is substituted for s, then s[i] denotes $a[m+i]$ for $i = 0 \ldots$ HIGH(s), where HIGH(s) $= n\text{-}m$.

13. Function procedures

So far we have encountered two possibilities to pass a result from a procedure body to its calling place: the result is either assigned to a non-local variable or to a variable parameter. There exists a third method: the function procedure. It permits the use of the computed result (as an intermediate value) in an expression. The function procedure identifier stands for a computation as well as for the computed result. The procedure declaration is characterized by the indication of the result's type behind the parameter list. As an example, we rephrase the power computation given above.

```
PROCEDURE power(x: REAL; i: CARDINAL): REAL;
  VAR z: REAL;
BEGIN z : = 1.0;
  WHILE i > 0 DO
    IF ODD(i) THEN z : = z*x END;
    x : = x*x; i : = i DIV 2
  END;
  RETURN z
END power
```

Possible calls are

```
u : = power(2.5, 3)
A[i] : = power(B[i], 2)
u : = x + power(y,i + 1)/power(z,i-1)
```

The statement which passes the result consists of the symbol RETURN followed by the expression specifying the result. *Return statements* may occur at several places in the procedure body and cause termination of its execution. Normally, however, the return statement is placed immediately preceding the closing symbol END. Return statements may also be used within normal procedures, in which case no expression follows the RETURN symbol. This facility may serve to signal unusual termination. Such a return statement is implied in the end of every procedure.

Calls inside an expression are called *function designators.* Their syntax is the same as that of procedure calls. However, a parameter list is mandatory, although it may be empty.

$ ReturnStatement = "RETURN" [expression].

We now revisit the previous example of adding the elements of an array and formulate it as a function procedure.

```
PROCEDURE sum(VAR a: Vector; n: CARDINAL): REAL;
  VAR i: CARDINAL; s: REAL;
BEGIN s : = 0.0;
  FOR i : = 0 TO n-1 DO
    s : = a[i] + s
  END ;
```

```
      RETURN s
    END sum
```

This procedure, as previously specified, sums the elements a[0] ... a[n-1], where n is given as a value parameter, and may be different from (but not larger than!) the number of elements N. A more elegant solution specifies a as an open array, omitting the explicit indication of the array's size.

```
    PROCEDURE sum(VAR x: ARRAY OF REAL): REAL;
      VAR i: CARDINAL; s: REAL;
    BEGIN s : = 0.0;
      FOR i : = 0 TO HIGH(s) DO
        s : =  x[i] + s
      END ;
      RETURN s
    END sum
```

Obviously, procedures are capable of generating more than one result by making assignments to several variables. Only one value, however, can be returned as the result of a function. This value, moreover, cannot be of a structured type. Therefore, the other results must be passed to the caller via VAR parameter or assignment to variables that are not local to the function procedure. Consider for example the following procedure which computes a primary result denoted as the function's value and a secondary result used to count the number of times the procedure is called.

```
    PROCEDURE square(x: CARDINAL): CARDINAL;
    BEGIN n : = n + 1;
      RETURN x*x
    END square
```

There is nothing remarkable about this example as long as the secondary result is used for its indicated purpose. However, it might be misused as follows:

```
    m : = square(m) + n
```

Here the secondary result occurs as an argument of the expression containing the function designator itself. The consequence is that e.g. the values

```
    square(m) + n   and   n + square(m)
```

differ, seemingly defying the basic law of commutativity of addition.

Assignments of values from within function procedures to non-local variables are called *side-effects*. The programmer should be fully aware of their capability of producing unexpected results when the function is used inappropriately.

We summarize:

1. A function procedure specifies a result which is used at its place of call as an argument of an expression.

2. The result of a function procedure cannot be structured.

3. If a function procedure generates secondary results, it is said to have side-effects. These must be used with care. It is advisable to use a regular procedure instead, which passes its results via VAR parameters.

4. We recommend to choose function identifiers which are nouns. The noun then denotes

the function's result. Boolean functions are appropriately labelled by an adjective. In contrast, regular procedures should be designated by a verb describing their action.

14. Recursion

Procedures may not only be called, but can call procedures themselves. Since any procedure that is visible can be called, a procedure may call itself. This self-reactivation is called *recursion*. Its use is appropriate when an algorithm is recursively defined and in particular when applied to a recursively defined data structure.

Consider as an example the task of listing all possible *permutations* of n distinct objects a[1] ... a[n]. Calling this operation Permute(n), we can formulate its algorithm as follows:

First, keep a[n] in its place and generate all permutations of a[1] ... a[n-1] by calling Permute(n-1), then repeat the same process after having exchanged a[n] with a[i] for i = 1. Continue repeating for all values i = 2 ... n-1. This recipe is formulated as a program as follows, using characters as permuted objects.

```
MODULE Permute;
FROM InOut IMPORT Read, Write, WriteLn;

VAR n: CARDINAL; ch: CHAR;
    a: ARRAY [1..20] OF CHAR;

PROCEDURE output;
 VAR i: CARDINAL;
BEGIN
 FOR i : = 1 TO n DO Write(a[i]) END ;
 WriteLn
END output;

PROCEDURE permute(k: CARDINAL);
 VAR i: CARDINAL; t: CHAR;
BEGIN
 IF k = 1 THEN output
 ELSE permute(k-1);
  FOR i : = 1 TO k-1 DO
   t : = a[i]; a[i] : = a[k]; a[k] : = t;
   permute(k-1);
   t : = a[i]; a[i] : = a[k]; a[k] : = t
  END
 END
END permute;

BEGIN Write(">"); n : = 0; Read(ch);
 WHILE ch > " " DO
  n : = n + 1; a[n] : = ch; Write(ch); Read(ch)
 END ;
 WriteLn; permute(n)
```

END Permute.

The data generated using 3 letters as objects are

ABC BAC CBA BCA ACB CAB

Every chain of recursive calls must terminate at some time, and hence every recursive procedure must place the recursive call within a conditional statement. In the example given above, the recursion terminates when the number of the objects to be permuted is 1.

The number of possible permutations can easily be derived from the algorithm's recursive definition. We express this number appropriately as a function np(n). Given n elements, there are n choices for the element a[n], and with each fixed a[n] we obtain np(n-1) permutations. Hence the total number np(n) = n∗np(n-1). Evidently np(1) = 1. The computation of np is now expressible as a recursive function procedure.

```
PROCEDURE np(n: CARDINAL): CARDINAL;
BEGIN
  IF n <= 1 THEN RETURN 1
  ELSE RETURN n * np(n-1)
  END
END np
```

We recognize np as the factorial function, which can also be expressed as

np(n) = 1∗2∗3∗ ... ∗n

This formula suggests to program the algorithm using repetition instead of recursion

```
PROCEDURE np(n: CARDINAL): CARDINAL;
  VAR p: CARDINAL;
BEGIN p := 1;
  WHILE n > 1 DO
    p := n∗p; n := n-1
  END ;
  RETURN p
END np
```

This formulation will compute the result more efficiently than the recursive version. The reason is that every call requires some "administrative" instructions whose execution costs time. The instructions representing repetition are less time-consuming. Although the difference may not be too relevant, it is recommended to employ a repetitive formulation in place of the recursive one, whenever this is easily possible. It is always possible in principle; however, the repetitive version may complicate and obscure the algorithm to such a degree that the advantages turn into disadvantages. For example, a repetitive form of the procedure permute is much less simple and obvious than the one shown above. To illustrate the usefulness of recursion, two additional examples follow. They typically stem from problems whose solution is naturally found and explained using recursion.

The first example belongs to the class of algorithms which operate on data whose structure is also defined recursively. The specific problem consists of converting simple expressions into their corresponding *postfix form*, i.e. a form in which the operator follows its operands. An expression shall here be defined using EBNF as follows:

```
expression = term {(" + "|"-") term}.
term = factor {("∗"|"/") factor}.
```

factor = letter | "(" expression")"|"[" expression "]".

Denoting terms as T0, T1, and factors as F0, F1, the rules of conversion are

```
T0 + T1        -->  T0 T1 +
T0 - T1        -->  T0 T1 -
F0 * F1        -->  F0 F1 *
F0 / F1        -->  F0 F1 /

(E)            -->  E
[E]            -->  E
```

The following program *Postfix* inputs expressions from the terminal and checks the input for syntactic correctness. It does so not by generating error messages in case of inappropriate input, but by echoing to the output medium only in case of correct input. As output operation a procedure *WriteChar* is imported not from the standard *Terminal*, but instead from a *WindowHandler*, supposed to represent so-called *windows* allocated on a display. We may think of each window as representing an individual output stream of characters. Our example uses one window to echo the accepted input, the other window for the converted expression, the genuine output.

The program truthfully mirrors the structure of the syntax of accepted expressions. As the syntax is recursive, so is the program. This close mirroring is the best guarantee for the program's correctness. Note also that similarly repetition in the syntax, expressed by the curly brackets, yields repetition in the program, expressed by while statements. No procedure in this program calls itself directly. Instead, recursion occurs indirectly by a call of expression on term, which calls factor, which calls expression. Indirect recursion is obviously much less visible than direct recursion.

This example also illustrates a case of local procedures. Notably, factor is declared local to term, and term local to expression, following the rule that objects should preferrably be declared local to the scope in which they are used. This rule may not only be advisable, but even crucial, as demonstrated by the variables addop (local to term) and mulop (local to factor). If these variables were declared globally, the program would fail. To find the explanation, we must recall the rule that local variables exist (and are allocated storage) during the time in which their procedure is active. An immediate consequence is that in the case of a recursive call, new incarnations of the local variables are created. Hence, there exist as many as there are levels of recursion. This also implies that a programmer must ensure that the depth of recursion never becomes inordinately large.

```
MODULE Postfix;
 FROM Terminal IMPORT Read;
 FROM WindowHandler IMPORT
  Window, OpenWindow, WriteChar, CloseWindow;

 CONST EOL = 36C;
 VAR ch: CHAR; done: BOOLEAN;
  w0,w1: Window;

 PROCEDURE expression;
  VAR addop: CHAR;

  PROCEDURE term;
```

```
    VAR mulop: CHAR;

    PROCEDURE factor;
    BEGIN
     IF ch = "(" THEN
       WriteChar(w0,ch); Read(ch); expression;
       WHILE ch # ")" DO Read(ch) END
     ELSIF ch = "[" THEN
       WriteChar(w0,ch); Read(ch); expression;
       WHILE ch # "]" DO Read(ch) END
     ELSE
       WHILE (ch < "a") OR (ch > "z") DO Read(ch) END ;
       WriteChar(w1,ch)
     END ;
     WriteChar(w0,ch); Read(ch)
    END factor;

   BEGIN (*term*) factor;
    WHILE (ch = "*") OR (ch = "/") DO
     WriteChar(w0,ch); mulop : = ch; Read(ch);
     factor; WriteChar(w1,mulop)
    END
   END term;

   BEGIN (*expression*)term;
    WHILE (ch = " + ") OR (ch = "-") DO
     WriteChar(w0,ch); addop : = ch; Read(ch);
     term; WriteChar(w1,addop)
    END
   END expression;

  BEGIN OpenWindow(w0, 50, 50, 300, 400, "input", done);
     OpenWindow(w1, 400, 100, 300, 400, "output", done);
   WriteChar(w0, ">"); Read(ch);
   WHILE ch > = EOL DO
    expression;
    WriteChar(w0, EOL); WriteChar(w1, EOL);
    WriteChar(w0, ">"); Read(ch)
   END ;
   CloseWindow(w1); CloseWindow(w0)
  END Postfix.
```

A sample of data processed and generated by this program is shown below.

> a + b	ab +
> a*b + c	ab*c +
> a + b*c	abc* +
> a*(b/[c-d])	abcd-/*

The next program example demonstration recursion belongs to the class of problems that search for a solution by trying and testing. A partial "solution" which is once "posted" may, after testing had shown its invalidity, have to be retracted. This kind of approach is therefore also called *backtracking*. Recursion is often very convenient for the formulation of such algorithms.

Our specific example is supposed to find all possible placement of 8 queens on a chess board in such a fashion that none is checking any other piece, i.e. each row, column, and diagonal must contain at most one piece. The approach consists of trying to place a queen in column j (starting with j=8) assuming that each column to the right contains a correctly placed queen already. If no place is free in column j, the next column to its right has to be reconsidered. The information necessary to deduce whether or not a given square is still free, is represented by the three global variables called *row, d1, d2* such that

row[i] & d1[i+j] & d2[N+i-j] = "the square in row i and column j is free"

The program uses a set of procedures imported from a module called *LineDrawing* to picture the output in an appealing graphical form. In particular, a call of

paint(c, x, y, w, h)

paints a rectangle with lower left corner at coordinates x, y and with width w and height h in "color" c. This procedure can evidently be used to draw lines between the fields of the chess board as well as to shade individual squares.

Recursion occurs directly in procedure TryCol. The auxiliary procedures PlaceQueen and RemoveQueen could in principle be declared local to TryCol. However, there exists a single chess board only (represented by row, d1, d2), and these procedures are appropriately considered as belonging to these global data, and hence not as local to (each incarnation of) TryCol.

```
MODULE Queens;
FROM LineDrawing IMPORT width, height, paint, clear;

CONST N = 8; (*no. of rows and columns*)
     L = 512; (*size of board*)
     M = L DIV N; (*size of squares*)

VAR x0, y0: CARDINAL; (*origin coordinates of board*)
   row: ARRAY [1..N] OF BOOLEAN;
      (*row[i] = "no queen on i-th row"*)
   d1:  ARRAY [2..2*N] OF BOOLEAN;
      (*d1[i] = "no queen on i-th upleft to lowright diagonal"*)
   d2:  ARRAY [1..2*N-1] OF BOOLEAN;
      (*d2[i] = "no queen on i-th lowleft to upright diagonal"*)

PROCEDURE ClearAndDrawBoard;
 VAR i,j,x,y: CARDINAL;
BEGIN clear(1);
 FOR i: = 1 TO N DO row[i] : = TRUE END ;
 FOR i: = 1 TO 2*N DO d1[i] : = TRUE END ;
 FOR i: = 1 TO 2*N-1 DO d2[i] : = TRUE END ;
 x0: = (width-L) DIV 2; x : = x0;
 y0 : = (height-L) DIV 2; y : = y0;
 paint(3, x0, y0, L, L);
 FOR i: = 0 TO N DO
```

```
    paint(0, x0, y, L, 2); y := y + M;
    paint(0, x, y0, 2, L); x := x + M;
  END
END ClearAndDrawBoard;

PROCEDURE pause;
 VAR n: CARDINAL;
BEGIN n := 50000;
 REPEAT n := n-1 UNTIL n = 0
END pause;

PROCEDURE PlaceQueen(i,j: CARDINAL);
BEGIN
 row[i] := FALSE; d1[i + j] := FALSE; d2[N + i-j] := FALSE;
 paint(0, x0 + 2 + (j-1)*M, y0 + 2 + (i-1)*M, M-2, M-2)
END PlaceQueen;

PROCEDURE RemoveQueen(i,j: CARDINAL);
BEGIN
 row[i] := TRUE; d1[i + j] := TRUE; d2[N + i-j] := TRUE;
 paint(3, x0 + 2 + (j-1)*M, y0 + 2 + (i-1)*M, M-2, M-2)
END RemoveQueen;

PROCEDURE TryCol(j: CARDINAL);
 VAR i: CARDINAL;
BEGIN i := N;
 REPEAT
  IF row[i] & d1[i + j] & d2[N + i-j] THEN
    PlaceQueen(i,j);
    IF j > 1 THEN TryCol(j-1)
     ELSE pause
    END ;
    RemoveQueen(i,j)
   END ;
   i := i-1
  UNTIL i = 0
END TryCol;

BEGIN ClearAndDrawBoard; TryCol(N); clear(3)
END Queens.
```

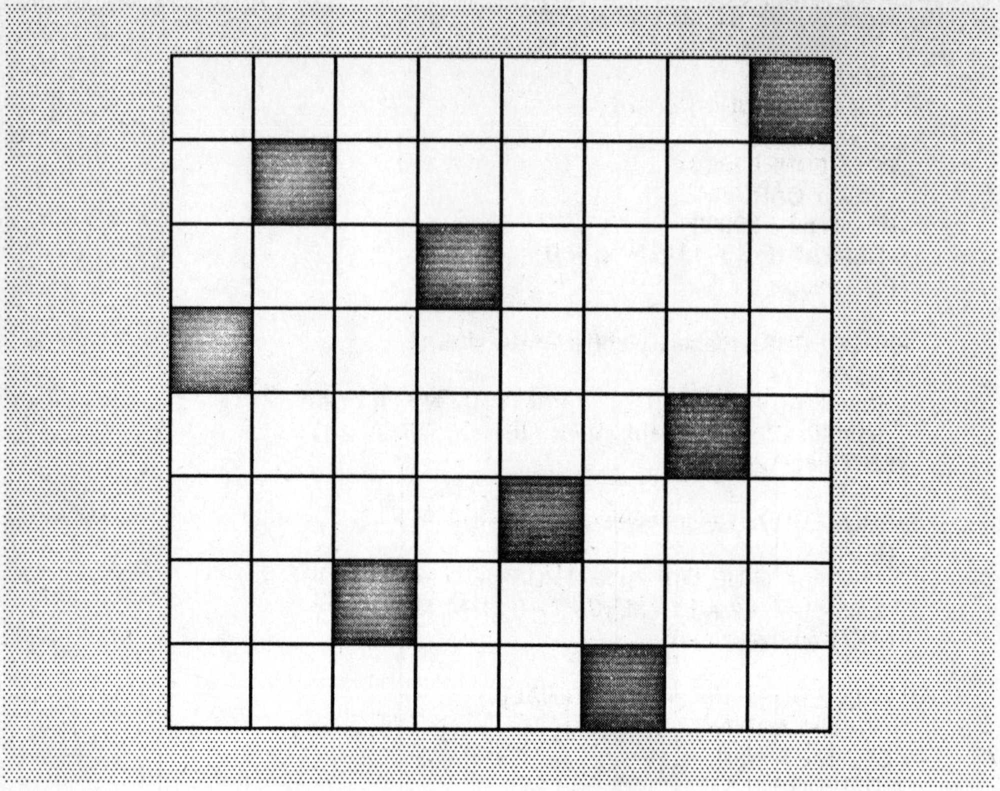

15. Type Declarations

Every variable declaration specifies the variable's type as its constant property. The type can be one of the standard, primitive types, or it may be of a type declared in the program itself. Type declarations have the form

\$ TypeDeclaration = identifier " = " type.

They are preceded by the symbol TYPE. Types are classified into *unstructured* and *structured types*. Each type essentially defines the set of values which a variable of this type may assume. A value of an unstructured type is an atomic unit, whereas a value of structured type has *components* (elements). For example, the type CARDINAL is unstructured; its elements are atomic. It does not make sense, e.g. to refer to the third bit of the value 13; the circumstance that a number may "have a third bit", or a second digit, is a characteristic of its (internal) representation, which intentionally is to remain unknown.

In the following sections we shall introduce ways to declare unstructured types and structured types. Apart from the standard types encountered so far, unstructured types may be declared as enumeration types or as subrange types. Among the structured types, we distinguish between various structuring methods of which we have so far encountered the array only. In addition, there exist set and record types. A facility to introduce structures that vary dynamically during program execution is based on the concept of pointers and will be discussed in a separate chapter.

\$ type = SimpleType | ArrayType | RecordType | SetType | PointerType | ProcedureType.
\$ SimpleType = qualident | enumeration | SubrangeType.

Before proceeding to the various kinds of types, we note that in general, if a type T is declared by the declaration

       TYPE T = someType

and a variable t is declared as

       VAR t: T

then these two declarations can always be merged into the single declaration

       VAR t: someType

However, in this case t's type has no explicit name and therefore remains anonymous.

The concept of type is important, because it divides a program's set of variables into disjoint classes. Inadvertent assignments among members of different classes can therefore be detected by a mere inspection of the program text without executing the program. Given, for example, the declarations

       VAR b: BOOLEAN;
         i: INTEGER;
         c: CARDINAL

the assignment b := i is impossible, because the types of b and i are incompatible. Two types are said to be *compatible,* if they are declared as equal or satisfy certain compatibility rules to be discussed subsequently. An important case of exceptional compatibility are the types INTEGER and CARDINAL. Hence, the assignment i := c is admissible.

To exhibit the rules of type compatibility, we assume the declarations

```
TYPE  A  =  ARRAY [0..99]  OF CHAR;
      B  =  ARRAY [0..99]  OF CHAR;
      C  =  A
```

In this case, variables of type A are assignable to those of type C (and vice versa), but not to those of type B. However, assignment of a[i] to b[j] is admissible, because they are both of the same type CHAR.

16. Enumeration types

A new unstructured type may be declared as an *enumeration*, i.e. by enumerating the set of values which belong to this type. The type declaration

$$T = (c1, c2, ... , cn)$$

introduces the new, unstructured type T, whose values are denoted by the n constant identifiers c1, c2, ... , cn. These are the only values belonging to that type. The syntax for the enumeration type declaration is

$ enumeration = "(" IdentList ")".

Operations on values of such type must be defined by programmer declared procedures. Apart from assignment, however, also comparison is possible. The values are ordered; the smallest is c1, the largest is cn. Examples of enumeration types are

```
TYPE color  = (red, orange, yellow, green, blue, violet);
     weekday = (Monday, Tuesday, Wednesday, Thursday, Friday, Saturday, Sunday);
     month   = (Jan, Feb, Mar, Apr, May, Jun, Jul, Aug, Sep, Oct, Nov, Dec)
```

The ordinal number of a constant ci can be obtained by application of the standard function ORD(ci), and it is i-1. For example:

ORD(red) = 0, ORD(Sunday) = 6, ORD(Dec) = 11.

The standard type BOOLEAN is also an enumeration type. It can be considered as having been specified by the declaration

BOOLEAN = (FALSE, TRUE)

17. Subrange types

If a variable is known (or supposed) to assume values within a certain contiguous range only, this fact can be specified by declaring it to be of a so-called *subrange* type. Assume, for example, that a variable i assumes values in the range from 1 up to (and including) N only, we specify

TYPE S = [1..N]

VAR i: S

(this can, of course, be abbreviated by VAR i: [1..N]).

Every subrange type has a *base type*, which is the type of its values. All operators defined for the base type also apply to the subrange type. The only restriction concerns the values that can be assigned to variables of the subrange type.

The syntax of a subrange type is

$ SubrangeType = "[" ConstExpression ".." ConstExpression "]".

where the expressions denote the limits of the range and must contain constants only.

Examples of subrange declarations are

letter = ["A" .. "Z"]
digit = ["0" .. "9"]
workday = [Monday .. Friday]

It is important to note the rules concerning the base type of numeric subranges: If the lower limit is negative, the base type is assumed INTEGER, otherwise CARDINAL. Also, no subrange may be defined on REAL numbers.

The use of subrange types has the advantage of offering additional safeguard against inadvertent value assignment and therefore may assist in detecting mistakes. Note, however, that these checks occur during program execution, as such errors cannot be detected by inspection of the program text only.

18. Set types

Every data type defines a set of values. In the case of a set type S, this set of values is the set of all possible sets consisting of elements from a given base type B. For example, if the base type B is the subrange

$$B = [0..1]$$

and the set type S is declared as

$$S = SET OF B$$

then the values of type S are the sets {}, {0}, {1}, {0,1}. If the base type has n distinct values, then its set type has 2 to the power of n values. {} denotes the empty set.

In a previous chapter, we have already encountered the standard set type BITSET. It is defined as

$$BITSET = SET OF [0..W-1]$$

where W is the wordlength of the computer used. Notably, the operations of set union, difference, and intersection, as well as the membership test IN are applicable to all set types, and not only to BITSET.

In order to make evident the type of a set constant, the set denoted by curly brackets must be preceded by the appropriate type identifier. It can be omitted in the case of the standard type BITSET.

The syntax of a set type declaration is

$ SetType = "SET" "OF" SimpleType.

The syntax of sets as they occur as operands in expressions, has been presented in the chapter of the standard type BITSET. We recall that it is formed by enclosing the list of elements by set brackets which are preceded by the identifier denoting the type of the set (which can be omitted in the case BITSET). Two restrictions pertaining to sets in Modula are important to remember:

1. Sets must contain constants only.

2. The base type of a set type must be an enumeration or a subrange. In addition, implementations of Modula are allowed to set a limit to the number of elements admissible in base types. That limit is usually the wordlength of the computer used, which is quite a small number, usually 16 or 32.

Although these rules restrict the generality of the set concept, set types are a powerful tool and allow to express operations on individual bits of an operand on a high level of abstraction based on a familiar and intuitively appealing mathematical concept. In order to mellow the severity of restriction 1 (and still retain the obtained simplicity and efficiency of set generators), two standard (generic) procedures are offered, where s must be a variable and x is an expression of the base type of s.

> INCL(s,x)   include element x in set s
>
> EXCL(s,x)   exclude element x from set s

An application of the type BITSET that does not directly reflect on the notion of a set, but has nevertheless become quite important and practical, shall be mentioned to conclude this chapter. It concerns the representation of the data for a raster scan display. These data are called a *bitmap,* because every single dot on the screen is represented by (mapped into) an individual bit in the computer's store, 1 denoting black and 0 denoting white (or vice-versa). Such a bitmap is conveniently described as an array of bitsets. Assume now that we are to represent a display screen with M lines each containing N dots for a computer with wordlength W. (We also assume that N is a multiple of W). The appropriate declaration is then

> VAR bitmap: ARRAY [0 .. M*(N DIV W)-1] OF BITSET

Painting the dot (picture element) at coordinate x,y is now expressed by the following procedure:

```
PROCEDURE PaintBlack(x,y : CARDINAL);
BEGIN
  INCL(bitmap[N*y + x DIV W], x MOD W)
END PaintBlack
```

A procedure MakeWhite would merely feature EXCL instead of INCL. Here we assume that N is a multiple of W, and that $0 <= x < N$ and $0 <= y < M$. If this is not guaranteed, appropriate tests should be included. Clearing the screen is achieved efficiently by assignments of empty sets to all elements of the bitmap array instead of setting individual bits.

> FOR i : = 0 TO M*(N DIV W)-1 DO bitmap[i] : = {} END

19. Record Types

In an array all elements are of the same type. In contrast to the array, the record structure offers the possibility to declare a collection of elements as a unit even if the elements are of different types. The following examples are typical cases where the record is the appropriate choice of structuring method. A date consists of three elements, namely day, month, and year. A description of a person may consist of the person's names, sex, identification number, and birthdate. This is expressed by the following type declarations

```
Date  =    RECORD day : [1 .. 31];
                mo: month;
                yr: CARDINAL
           END

Person = RECORD
               firstName, lastName: ARRAY [0 .. 23] OF CHAR;
               male: BOOLEAN;
               idno: CARDINAL;
               birth: Date
           END
```

The record structure makes it possible to refer either to the entire collection of data or to individual elements. Elements of a record are also called *record fields,* and their names are called *field identifiers.* This stems from the habit of looking at such data as forms or tables drawn on paper with individual fields delineated as rectangles and labelled with field names. Similar to arrays, where we denote the i-th element of an array a by a[i], i.e. by the array identifier followed by an index, we denote the field f of a record r by r.f , i.e. by the record identifier followed by the field's name. Given the variables

```
d1, d2 :  Date;
p1, p2 :  Person;
student:  ARRAY [0 .. 99] OF Person
```

we can construct the following variable designators:

```
d1.day
d2.mo
p1.firstName
p1.birth
```

These examples show that fields may themselves be structured. Similarly, records may be elements of array or record structures, i.e. there exists the possibility to construct hierarchies of structures. As a consequence, selectors of elements can be sequenced, as shown by the following examples of designators. The multi-dimensional array discussed in the chapter on arrays now appears as a particular case of these structuring hierarchies.

```
p1.lastName[7]
p2.birth.yr
```

```
student[23].idno
student[k].firstName[0]
```

At first sight the record may appear as a generalized array, because it relaxes the restriction that all elements be of the same type. However, in another aspect it is *more* restrictive than the array: the selector of the element must be a fixed field identifier, whereas the index selecting an array element may be an expression, i.e. a result of previous computations.

It is important to note that a record may assume arbitrary combinations of its field's values. Hence, in the example of the type Date, a value day = 31 may coexist with mo = Feb, although this is not an actual date.

The syntax of a record declaration is defined as follows.

```
$   RecordType  ="RECORD"
$                   FieldListSequence
$                "END".
$   FieldListSequence  =  FieldList {";" FieldList}.
$   FieldList  =  [IdentList ":" type | VariantFieldList ].
```

and that of a designator is

```
$   designator  =  qualident {selector} .
$   selector  =  "." identifier | "[" ExpList "]" | "↑".
```
Note: Variant field lists and the selector ↑ will be discussed later.

In order to express the processing of array elements conveniently, we had introduced the for statement. Similarly, we now introduce a statement which serves to process record fields in a convenient notation. Because record fields have their individual types, they in general also require to distinct operations, and hence the processing of a record cannot be expressed as a repetition of the same operation applied to the individual fields. Instead, the appropriate form is rather a sequence of individual statements involving the respective record fields. Since they all belong to one and the same record, the statement sequence can be subjected to a *with clause,* thereby forming a so-called *with statement.* The with clause specifies the record variable, and its effect is to qualify that record in the sense that its field identifiers may occur (within the statement sequence) by themselves, i.e. without being prefixed by the record identifier and the period. For example

```
WITH d1 DO
   day : = 10; mo : = Sep; yr : = 1981
END
```

is equivalent to

```
d1.day : = 10; d1.mo : = Sep; d1.yr : = 1981
```

The syntax of the WITH statement is

```
$   WithStatement =   "WITH" designator "DO"
$                     StatementSequence
$                     "END".
```

Apart from a possibly more concise notation, the with statement may offer the advantage of improved efficiency, in particular if the designator in the with clause contains array indices. These are evaluated once only, and therefore the following rule should be observed:

No assignments to variables occuring in the with clause should be made within the statement sequence, except of course to the fields of the designated record.

This rule is similar to the restriction of the for statement prohibiting assignments to the objects specified in the for clause. The programmer should be aware that this rule is a recommendation for good style. If it is violated, the effects are, if not undefined, difficult to understand and obscure. Moreover, the programmer should not expect a compiler to discover such violations.

20. Records with variant parts

Record types offer yet another kind of flexibility. A given record may assume various variant forms. This implies that the number and kind of fields may differ among different variables although they are of the same record type. It is obvious that this flexibility also gives rise to programming errors that are difficult to detect. In particular, it is now possible to assume in some part of a program that a variable is of a certain variant, whereas it actually is of another variant. This facility is therefore to be used with great caution.

The variant facility is illustrated by the following example:

```
Person =
RECORD
  lastName, firstName: Name;
  CASE male: BOOLEAN OF
    TRUE:   MilitaryRank: CARDINAL |
    FALSE:  maidenName: Name
  END ;
  idno:  CARDINAL;
  birth:  Date ;
  CASE state: MaritalStatus  OF
    single:  |
    married:  spouse: CARDINAL;
            NoOfChildren: CARDINAL;
            wedding: Date |
    widowed:  death: Date
  END
END
```

This example consists of five field lists, two of which are variant lists. They are formed according to the syntax

```
$   VariantFieldList =
$     "CASE" [identifier ":"] qualident "OF"
$       variant {"|" variant }
$       ["ELSE" FieldListSequence]
$     "END".
$   variant = CaseLabelList ":" FieldListSequence.
$   CaseLabelList = CaseLabels {"," CaseLabels}.
$   CaseLabels = ConstExpression [".." ConstExpression].
```

The variant list consists of a case clause followed by the various field lists, separated by the symbol "|". The meaning of a variant field list is that only that field list is applicable which is labelled by the current value of the (non-variant) field specified in the case clause. This field is called the *discriminator* or the *tag field*.

Referring to the above example, and given variables p1 and p2 of that type, the designator *p1.maidenName* is applicable only if p1.male = FALSE, i.e. if p1 represents a female person. Similarly, *p2.wedding* applies only if p2.state = married, i.e. if p2 represents a married person. The tag field serves as a discriminator between the various variants, and plays an important role in reducing the danger of the error of referring to inappropriate fields such as, e.g., to *p1.spouse* if p1.state = single. The likelihood of error is further reduced, if the correctness of a field's use is made evident through appropriate program structure. To this end, we introduce the so-called *case statement* which is used to distinguish between several cases. It can be considered as a generalization of the if statement, allowing for more than two cases. Its syntax is defined as

```
$  CaseStatement =
$     "CASE" expression "OF"
$         case {"|" case}
$         ["ELSE" StatementSequence ]
$     "END".
$  case = CaseLabelList ":" StatementSequence.
```

The similarity between the syntax of the case statement and that of the variant field list is noteworthy and mirrors their close relationship. This is illustrated by the following example which generates a readable listing of the data represented by a variable

```
resident : ARRAY [1..N] OF Person
```

We draw attention to the similarity of the structure of the type declaration and the structure of the program. The array consists of records containing variant parts; the for statement consists of a with statement containing case statements.

```
FOR i := 1 TO N DO
  WITH resident [i] DO
    WriteString(lastName); Write(" ");
    WriteString(firstName);
    CASE male OF
      TRUE:  WriteString (" male, military rank = ");
          WriteCard (MilitaryRank, 4) |
      FALSE: WriteString(" female, maiden name: ");
          WriteString(maidenName)
    END;
    WriteCard(idno, 8); WriteDate(birth); WriteLn;
    CASE state OF
      single:  WriteString(" single") |
      married: WriteString(" married");
            WriteCard(spouseId, 10);
            WriteCard(NoOfChildren, 4);
            WriteDate(wedding) |
      widowed: WriteString(" widowed");
            WriteDate(death)
    END
  END ;
  WriteLn
END
```

The case statement may, of course, also be used without attachment to variant records. However, it should only be used in situations where the values occurring as case labels are essentially adjacent. We demonstrate this rule of style by a negative example; it shows how the case statement should *not* be used.

```
CASE i*j OF
   1: S1 |
  11: S2 |
 121: S3
ELSE S4
END
```

Here a formulation using an if statement is much preferrable. In particular, the ELSE clause should be reserved for exceptional cases, i.e. those that are neither numerous among the possible cases nor do occur frequently during program execution.

21. Dynamic data structures and pointers

Array, record and set structures share the common property that they are *static*. This implies that variables of such a structure maintain the same structure during the whole time of their existence. In many applications, this is an intolerable restriction; they require data which do not only change their value, but also their composition, size, and structure. Typical examples are lists and trees that grow and shrink *dynamically*. Instead of providing list and tree structures, a collection that for some applications would again not suffice, Modula offers a basic tool to construct arbitrary structures. This is the *pointer type*.

Every complex data structure ultimately consists of elements whose structure is static. Pointers, i.e. values of pointer types, are themselves not structured, but rather are used to establish relationships among those static elements, usually called *nodes*. We also say that pointers link elements or point to elements. Evidently, different pointer variables may point to the same element, hence providing the possibility to compose arbitrarily complex structures, and at the same time opening many pitfalls for programming mistakes that are difficult to pinpoint. Operating with pointers indeed requires utmost care.

Pointers in Modula cannot point to arbitrary variables. The type of variable to which they point must be specified in the pointer type's declaration, and the pointer type is said to be *bound* to the referenced object's type. Example:

```
TYPE NodePtr = POINTER TO Node
VAR p0, p1: NodePtr
```

Here *NodePtr* (and thereby also variables p0 and p1) are bound to the type Node, i.e. they can point to variables of type Node only. These variables are, however, not created by the declaration of p0 and p1. Instead, they are created by a call of the standard procedure NEW. Specifically, the statement NEW(p0) creates a variable of type Node and assigns a pointer pointing to that variable (i.e. a value of type NodePtr) to p0. The created variable is said to be *dynamically created* (allocated); it has no name, is anonymous, and can be accessed only via a pointer using the *dereferencing operator* ↑. The said variable is denoted by the designator p0↑.

$ PointerType = "POINTER" "TO" type.

What really makes pointers such a powerful tool is the circumstance that they may point to variables which themselves contain pointers. This reminds us of procedures that call procedures and thereby introduce recursion. In fact, pointers are the tool to implement recursively defined data structures (such as lists and trees). The nature of the recursive data structure is evident from the declaration of the type of its elements.

Just as every recursion of procedure activation must terminate at some time, so must every recursion in referencing terminate at some point. The role of the if statement to terminate procedural recursion is here taken by the special pointer value NIL terminating referencing recursion. NIL points to no object. Alternatively, we may regard every pointer type as being a record with two variants, one pointing at objects of the specified, bound type, the other pointing at no object, i.e. having NIL as the only value. It is an obvious consequence that a designator of the form p↑ must never be evaluated, if p = NIL.

We summarize the following essential points.

1. Every pointer type is bound to a type; its values are pointers which point to variables of that type.

2. The referenced variables are anonymous and can be accessed via pointers only.

3. The referenced variables are dynamically created by the statement NEW(p) which assigns the variable's pointer to p.

4. The pointer constant NIL belongs to every pointer type and points to no object.

5. The variable referenced by a pointer p is denoted by the designator p↑. In order for p↑ to be meaningful, p must not have the value NIL.

Lists, also called *linear lists* or *chains,* are characterized by consisting of nodes that each have exactly one element which is a pointer (to the same type of nodes) itself, thereby implying recursion. Node types are typically records; a list pointer declaration then assumes the characteristic form

```
ListPtr  =  POINTER TO ListNode

ListNode =
RECORD
  key: CARDINAL;
  Data: ...
  next: ListPtr
END
```

"Data" actually stands for any number of fields representing data pertaining to the listed node. Key is part of these data; it is mentioned separately here because it is quite common to associate with each element a unique identifying key, and also because it will be used in subsequent examples of operations on lists. The essential ingredient here, however, is the field *next,* so labelled because it evidently is the pointer to the next element in the list. Direct recursion in data type declarations is not permitted for the obvious reason that there would be no evident termination. The declaration given above cannot be abbreviated into

```
List  =
RECORD
  key: CARDINAL; ...
  next: List
END
```

Assume now that a list is accessible in a program via its first element, denoted by the pointer variable

```
first: ListPtr
```

The empty list is represented by first = NIL. A longer list is most conveniently constructed by inserting new elements at its front. The following assignments are needed to insert one element (p is an auxiliary variable of type ListPtr)

```
NEW(p);
WITH p↑ DO
  (* assign values to key and data *)
  next : = first
END;
```

```
first : = p
```

Having constructed a list by repeated insertion of nodes, we may wish to *search the list* for a node with key value equal to a given x. We evidently use a repetition; the while statement is appropriate, because we do not know the number of nodes (and hence repetitions) beforehand. It is wise to include the case of the empty list!

```
p : = first;
WHILE (p # NIL) & (p↑.key # x) DO
  p : = p↑.next
END ;
IF p # NIL THEN found END
```

We draw attention to the fact that here we make use of the rule that b is not evaluated, if in the expression a & b the factor a is found to be FALSE. If this rule would not hold, the factor p↑.key # x might be evaluated with p = NIL, which is illegal.

Deletion of an element is particularly simple in the case of the first node:

```
p : = first; first : = p↑.next; DISPOSE(p)
```

DISPOSE is a standard procedure like NEW. It returns the storage space allocated to the variable p↑. Great care in its use is mandatory: had the pointer to this variable previously been assigned to other variables, these would now point to a non-existing object. The programmer should not expect this mistake to be automatically detected by a system.

NEW and DISPOSE are actually mere abbreviations for calls of procedures which handle storage allocation and deallocation. These procedures must be made available like those for input and output. Therefore, any program using NEW or DISPOSE must include in its heading the so-called import clause

```
FROM Storage IMPORT ALLOCATE, DEALLOCATE;
```

assuming that the two procedures are available from a module called Storage.

The second frequently encountered dynamic data structure is the *tree.* It is characterized by its nodes having n pointer fields each, where n is the degree of the tree. The common and in some sense optimal case is the binary tree with n = 2. The respective declarations are

```
TreePtr  = POINTER TO TreeNode;
TreeNode =
  RECORD
    key: CARDINAL;
    data: ...
    left, right: TreePtr
  END
```

The place of the variable first in the case of lists is taken by a variable to be called

```
root: TreePtr
```

with root = NIL implying the empty tree. Trees are commonly used to represent collections of data in order of ascending key values, making retrieval very efficient. The following statements represent a *search in an ordered binary tree,* whose similarity to the binary search in an ordered array is remarkable. Again, p is an auxiliary variable (of type TreePtr).

```
p : = root;
```

```
WHILE (p # NIL) & (p↑.key # x) DO
  IF p↑.key < x THEN p : = p↑.right
  ELSE p : = p↑.left
  END
END ;
IF p # NIL THEN found END
```

This example is a repetitive version of the tree search. Next we show the recursive version. It is, in addition, extended such that a new node is created and *inserted* at the appropriate place, whenever no node with key value equal to x exists.

```
PROCEDURE search(VAR p: TreePtr; x: CARDINAL): TreePtr;
BEGIN
  IF p # NIL THEN
    IF p↑.key < x THEN
      RETURN search (p↑.right, x)
    ELSIF p↑.key > x THEN
      RETURN search (p↑.left, x)
    ELSE
      RETURN p
    END
  ELSE (*not found, hence insert*)
    NEW(p);
    WITH p↑ DO
      key : = x;  left : = NIL;  right : = NIL
    END ;
    RETURN p
  END
END search
```

The call search(root,x) now stands for a search of the tree represented by the variable root.

And this concludes our examples of operations on lists and trees to illustrate pointer handling. Lists and trees have nodes which are all of the same type. We draw attention to the fact that the pointer facility admits the construction of even more general data structure consisting of nodes of various types. Typical for all these structures is that all nodes are declared as record types. Hence, the record emerges as a particularly useful data structure in conjunction with pointers.

Creation and removal of nodes is expressed by the two standard procedures NEW and DISPOSE, which are part of a system's storage management. Sometimes it may be more efficient, if a program handles its storage by itself. This can be done quite easily by maintaining, for each node type that occurs in the program, a list of nodes that otherwise would have been disposed of. This list of available nodes is then inspected each time a new node is needed:

```
PROCEDURE NewNode(VAR p: NodePtr);
BEGIN
  IF avail = NIL THEN NEW(p)
  ELSE p : = avail; avail : = p↑.next
  END
END NewNode
```

The drawback of such "personal storage management" is that storage is not traded among the various lists of dead nodes, if several exist.

22. Procedure types

So far, we have regarded procedures exclusively as program parts, i.e. as texts that specify actions to be performed on variables whose values are numbers, logical values, characters, etc. However, we may take the view that procedures themselves are objects that can be assigned to variables. In this light, a procedure declaration appears as a special kind of constant declaration, the value of this constant being a procedure. If we allow variables in addition to constants, it must be possible to declare types whose values are procedures. These are called *procedure types.*

A procedure type declaration specifies the number and the types of parameters and, if it is to be a function procedure, the type of the result. For example, a procedure type with one REAL argument and a result of the same type is declared by

       Func = PROCEDURE (REAL): REAL

and one with two arguments of type CARDINAL as

       Proc2 = PROCEDURE (CARDINAL, CARDINAL)

The general syntax is

```
$   ProcedureType  =  "PROCEDURE" [FormalTypeList].
$   FormalTypeList =
$      "(" [["VAR"] FormalType {"," ["VAR"] FormalType}] ")" [":" identifier].
```

If we now declare variables, for instance

       f: Func;
       p: Proc2

assignments such as

       f : = sin; p : = WriteCard

are possible. Subsequently the call p(x,6) will be equivalent to WriteCard(x,6), and f(x) is equivalent to sin(x).

It is now also possible to declare procedures which have procedures as parameters. Consider, for example, the task to perform a certain action, i.e. to execute a procedure, for each element of a binary tree. The solution is appropriately formulated by a (recursive) procedure expressing the *traversal of the tree* and calling, for each tree node visited, the required procedure which is supplied as a parameter and is therefore called a *formal procedure.*

```
       PROCEDURE TraverseTree(p: TreePtr; Q: Proc2);
       BEGIN
         IF p # NIL THEN
           TraverseTree (p↑.left, Q);
           Q(p↑.key, 6);
```

```
        TraverseTree (p↑.right, Q)
    END
    END TraverseTree
```

If we now call

```
    TraverseTree(root, WriteCard)
```

the key values of all nodes will be written in sequence of the ordering of the tree. The same procedure may be used to write these values in octal form, for example, by the call

```
    TraverseTree(root, WriteOct)
```

It should be evident from this example, that, although procedure types are used rarely, they constitute a powerful facility.

To conclude, we emphasize the restriction that procedures that are assigned to variables or are passed as parameters, must not be declared local to any other procedure. Neither can they be standard procedures (such as ODD, INCL, etc.).

23. Modules

Modules are the most important feature distinguishing Modula-2 from its ancestor, Pascal. We have already encountered modules, simply because every program is a module. However, most programs are partitioned into *several* modules, each module containing constants, variables, procedures, and perhaps types. Objects declared in other modules can be referenced in a module M, if they are explicitly made to be known in M, i.e. if they are imported into M. In the examples of the preceding chapters, we have typically imported procedures for input and output from modules containing collections of frequently used procedures. These procedures are actually part of our program, even if we have not programmed them and they are textually disjoint.

The key point is that modules can be kept in a program "library" and are automatically referenced when a programmer's program is loaded and executed. Hence it is possible to prepare collections of frequently used operations (such as for input and output), and to avoid reprogramming them each time a program needs such operations. Sophisticated implementations go even one step further and offer what is called *separate compilation*. This signifies that such modules are not stored in the program library in source form as Modula texts, but rather in compiled form. Upon program loading, the compiled (main) program is joined (linked) with the precompiled modules from which it imports objects. In this case, the compiler must also have access to descriptions of the objects of the previously compiled, imported modules, when the importing program is compiled. This facility distinguishes separate compilation from independent compilation as it exists in typical implementations of Fortran, Pascal, and assembler codes.

Every subsidiary module may again import objects from other modules. A program therefore constitutes an entire hierarchy of modules. The main program is said to be at the highest *level,* those modules which do not import objects at all being at the lowest level. Usually, a programmer is not even aware of this hierarchy, because his programs (modules) import objects from modules that he has not programmed himself; therefore he is unaware of their imports and of the module hierarchy below them. In principle, however, his program is the text written by himself, extended with the texts of the imported modules.

These extensions are usually quite large (even if the direct imports consist of a few output procedures only). In principle, the indirect imports constitute the entire so-called *environment* or operating system. In a single-user computer system, there is virtually no need for any parts that are neither directly nor indirectly imported by the main program. However, some modules, such as the basic input/output and file system, may be required by all programs and therefore become de facto resident and may therefore be regarded as the operating system.

The principal motivation behind the partitioning of a program into modules is - beside the use of modules provided by other programmers - the establishment of a *hierarchy of abstractions.* For example, in the previously encountered cases of imported input/output procedures, we merely wish to have them available, but do not need to know - or rather do not wish to bother to learn - how these procedures function in detail. To abstract means to "take away" from the essentials and thereby to ignore certain details. Each module constitutes an abstraction, if we regard it from "the outside". We even wish to go one step further: we wish not only to ignore the details of its innards, but to *hide* them. The primary reason for this wish is that if the innards are protected from outside access, we can guarantee their correct functioning, thereby being able to limit the area of error search in the case of a malfunctioning program. The secondary, but not less important reason is to make it possible to change (improve) the innards of imported modules without having to change (and/or recompile) the importing modules. This effective decoupling of modules is indispensible for the development of large programs, in particular, if modules are developed by different people, and if we regard the operating system as the low section of a program's module hierarchy. Without decoupling, any change or correction in an operating system or in library modules would become virtually impossible.

A direct consequence of this need for decoupling is the necessity for a textual separation of the essentials from the details. The essentials of a module are the data about objects that are importable into other modules; the details are those parts that are to be hidden and protected. In Modula-2, this separation is achieved by dividing subsidiary modules into a *definition part* and an *implementation part*, and by enumerating the objects that are to be visible outside the module in an explicit *export list.* The definition part contains this export list and the declarations of the exported objects; it must be considered like a prefix to the implementation part. An importer of a module needs to have available the definition part only, the implementation part remains the property of the module's designer. As long as he alters the implementation part only (in a sensible way), he need not report his activity to the users (clients) of his module. Both parts are compiled separately, and are therefore called *compilation units.*

Concluding this introduction to the module concept, we postulate that adequate implementations provide full type compatibility checking between objects, independent of whether these objects are declared in the same or in different modules, i.e. the checking mechanism of the compiler functions also across module boundaries. However, the programmer must realize that this checking provides no absolute safeguard against mistakes. After all, it concerns formal, syntactic aspects only; it does not cover the semantics. It would not detect, for instance, the replacement of the algorithm for the sine function by that of the cosine procedure. However, it must not be regarded as the duty of a compiler to protect programmers against ill-willed "colleagues".

24. Definition and implementation parts

A definition part of a module is called a *definition module*. It contains the list of exported objects and their declarations. These may be any kind of objects, but a few additional rules must be mentioned.

Concerning variables, we note that a module is a partition of an entire program text. Variables declared in a definition module therefore are global in the sense that they exist during the entire lifetime of the program, although they are visible and accessible only in those modules which import them. In the other modules they are invisible.

Procedure declarations in definition modules consist of a heading only. The procedure body belongs to the corresponding implementation module.

If a type is declared in a definition module, the full details of its declaration are visible in importing modules. If an enumeration or record type is declared, the export of its name automatically also causes the export of the identifiers of the enumerated constants or of the declared record fields. This *transparent export* stands in contrast to *opaque export* of a type. Opaque export is achieved by merely declaring the type's name in the definition module and hiding the full declaration in the implementation part. Opaque export is essentially restricted to pointer types. This constitutes an important case, however, because pointers are bound to another (usually a record) type which can be hidden. Examples which illustrate the hiding of details of data types, also known as "data abstraction" will follow later.

The following simple example exhibits the essential characteristics of modules, although typically modules are considerably larger pieces of program and contain a longer list of declarations. This example exports two procedures, *put* and *get*, adding data to and fetching data from a buffer which is hidden. Effectively, the buffer can only be accessed through these two procedures; it is therefore possible to guarantee the buffer's proper functioning.

```
DEFINITION MODULE Buffer;
  EXPORT QUALIFIED put, get, nonempty, nonfull;

  VAR nonempty, nonfull: BOOLEAN;
  PROCEDURE put(x: CARDINAL);
  PROCEDURE get(VAR x: CARDINAL);
END Buffer.
```

This definition part contains all the information about the buffer that a client is supposed to know. The details of its operation, its realization, are contained in the corresponding implementation module.

```
IMPLEMENTATION MODULE Buffer;
  CONST N = 100;
  VAR in, out: [0..N-1];
    n: [0..N];
```

```
buf: ARRAY [0..N-1] OF CARDINAL;

PROCEDURE put(x: CARDINAL);
BEGIN
 IF n < N THEN
   buf[in] : = x; in : = (in + 1) MOD N;
   n : = n + 1; nonfull : = n < N; nonempty : = TRUE
 END
END put;

PROCEDURE get(VAR x: CARDINAL);
BEGIN
 IF n > 0 THEN
   x : = buf[out]; out : = (out + 1) MOD N;
   n : = n-1; nonempty : = n > 0; nonfull : = TRUE
 END
END get;

BEGIN (*initialize*) n : = 0; in : = 0; out : = 0;
 nonempty : = FALSE; nonfull : = TRUE
END Buffer.
```

The example implements a fifo (first in first out) queue. This fact is not evident from the definition module; normally the semantics are mentioned in the form of a comment or other documentation. Such comments will usually explain what the module performs, but not how this is achieved. Therefore, different implementations may be provided for the same definition module. The differences may lie in the details of the mechanism; for example, the buffer might be represented as a linked list instead of an array (allocating buffer portions as needed, hence not limiting the buffer's size). Or, the differences may even lie in the semantics. The following program implements a stack (i.e. a lifo queue) instead of a fifo queue, nevertheless fitting the same definition part. Any change in a module's semantics necessitates corresponding adjustments in the module's clients, and must therefore be made with utmost care.

```
IMPLEMENTATION MODULE Buffer;
    ...........

PROCEDURE put(x: CARDINAL);
BEGIN
 IF n < N THEN
   buf[n] : = x; n : = n + 1; nonfull : = n < N; nonempty : = TRUE
 END
END put;

PROCEDURE get(VAR x: CARDINAL);
BEGIN
 IF n > 0 THEN
   n : = n-1; x : = buf[n]; nonempty : = n > 0; nonfull : = TRUE
 END
END get;
```

```
       BEGIN n : = 0; nonempty : = FALSE; nonfull : = TRUE
       END Buffer.
```

Evidently, nonempty is the precondition for get, and nonfull is the precondition of put. This concludes the introductory example.

The syntax of definition modules is

```
$   DefinitionModule =
$     "DEFINITION" "MODULE" identifier ";"
$       {import}
$       [export]
$       {definition}
$     "END" identifier "." .


$   definition = "CONST" {ConstantDeclaration ";"} |
$       "TYPE" {identifier [" = " type] ";"}  |
$       "VAR" {VariableDeclaration ";" }  |
$       ProcedureHeading ";".
```

The syntax of implementation parts is equal to that of main programs, except that the symbol IMPLEMENTATION is added to signal that there exists a corresponding definition part, whose declarations are automatically considered as belonging to the module.

```
$   ProgramModule =
$     "MODULE" identifier [priority] ";"
$       {import}
$       block identifier.


$   CompilationUnit = DefinitionModule |
$     ["IMPLEMENTATION"] ProgramModule.
```

The export list contains all the identifiers to be known outside the module. The significance of the symbol QUALIFIED will be explained in the later chapter on local modules. It is mandatory in definition modules. Normally, the list contains all identifiers declared in the definition module, and then merely serves for a redundancy check.

```
$   export = "EXPORT" ["QUALIFIED"] IdentList ";" .
```

Both definition and implementation parts may contain (several) import lists. The definition module should import those items only that are actually needed in the definition part itself. This minimizes its dependence on other modules.

```
$   import = ["FROM" identifier] "IMPORT" IdentList ";" .
```

The identifier following the symbol FROM is a module identifier and specifies the imported items' source. Without such a qualification we can only import module names (a relaxation of this rule will be explained in the chapter on local modules). If a module name is imported, all identifiers of that module's export list are automatically also imported. However, they need to be qualified like a record's field identifiers by the module's name. For example, if a module M exports a, b, c, the specification IMPORT M in a module N means that these objects can be referenced in N by the designators M.a, M.b, M.c. This facility permits to import different objects with the same name from different modules and to avoid conflicts of names. M then acts as a so-called *qualifying identifier*.

Standard identifiers are automatically imported into all modules.

The possibility to publicize a module in the form of its definition part and at the same time to retain its operational details hidden in its implementation part, is particularly convenient for the establishment of program libraries. Such collections of standard routines belong to every programming environment. They typically include routines for input and output operations, for file handling, and for the computation of mathematical functions. Although there exists no rigid standard for Modula, the modules InOut, RealInOut, LineDrawing, MathLib0, and Streams (or an equivalent thereof) can be considered as standard modules available in all implementations of Modula. These modules are introduced in subsequent chapters. Here we present the definition part of MathLib0 as a first example.

```
DEFINITION MODULE MathLib0;
  EXPORT QUALIFIED sqrt, exp, ln, sin, cos, arctan, real, entier;

  PROCEDURE sqrt(x: REAL): REAL;
  PROCEDURE exp(x: REAL): REAL;
  PROCEDURE ln(x: REAL): REAL;
  PROCEDURE sin(x: REAL): REAL;
  PROCEDURE cos(x: REAL): REAL;
  PROCEDURE arctan(x: REAL): REAL;
  PROCEDURE real(x: INTEGER): REAL;
  PROCEDURE entier(x: REAL): INTEGER;
END MathLib0.
```

25. Program decomposition into modules

The quality of a program has many aspects and is an elusive property. A user of a program may judge it according to its efficiency, reliability, or convenience of user dialog. Whereas efficiency can be expressed in terms of numbers, convenience of usage is rather a matter of personal judgement, and all too often a program's usage is called convenient as long as it is conventional. An engineer of a program may judge its quality according to its clarity and perspicuity, again rather elusive and subjective properties. However, if a property cannot be expressed in terms of precise numbers, this is no reason for classifying it as irrelevant. In fact, program clarity is enormously important, and to demonstrate (prove?) a program's correctness is ultimately a matter of convincing a person that the program is trustworthy. How can we approach this goal? After all, complicated tasks usually do inherently require complex algorithms, and this implies a myriad of details. And the details are the jungle in which the devil hides.

The only salvation lies in structure. A program must be decomposed into partitions which can be considered one at a time without too much regard for the remaining parts. At the lowest level the elements of the structure are statements, at the next level procedures, and at the highest level modules. In parallel with program structuring proceeds the structuring of data into arrays, records, etc. at the lower levels, and through association of variables with procedures and modules at the higher levels. The essence of programming is finding the right (or at least an appropriate) structure, and the experienced programmer is the person who has the intuition to find it at the stage of initial conception instead of during a gradual process of improvements and modifications. Yet, the programmer who has the courage to restructure when a better solution emerges is still much better off than the one who resigns and elaborates a program on the basis of a clearly inadequate structure, for this leads to those products that no one else, and ultimately not even the originator himself can "understand".

Even if there does not exist a recipe to determine the optimal structure of a program, there have emerged some criteria for guidance in the process of finding good and avoiding bad structure. A basic rule is that decomposition should be such that the connections between partitions are simple or "thin". A perhaps oversimplifying criterion for the thickness of a connection - also called *interface* - between two parts is the number of items that take part in it. Specifically, the interface of two modules is sketched in terms of the module's import lists, and a measure for the interface's thickness is the number of imported items. Hence, we must find a modularization which makes the import lists short. Naturally, it is difficult to find an optimum, for, the import lists would be shortest, i.e. they would disappear if the entire program were collapsed into a single module: a clearly undesirable solution.

The distinctive property of the module as the largest structuring unit is its capability to hide details and thereby to establish a new level of abstraction. This property is used in several forms; we can distinguish between the following typical cases.

1. The module separates two kinds of data representation and contains the collection of procedures that perform the data conversion between the two levels. The typical example

is a module for conversion of numbers from their abstract, atomic representation into sequences of decimal digits and vice-versa. Such modules contain no data of their own, they are typically packages of procedures.

2. The module's essence is a set of data. It hides the details of the data representation by granting access to these data through calls of its exported procedures only. An example of this case is a module which contains a data set storing individual items organized in a way that access to these items via key is fast. Another is a module whose hidden data set is a disk store; it hides the peculiar details necessary to operate the disk drive.

3. The module exports a data type and exports its associated operations. Typically, in Modula such a module exports one or several types in opaque mode (sometimes these are also called *private types*). It thereby hides the details of the data type's structure and also the details of the operations. By hiding them, it is possible to guarantee the validity of postulated invariant properties of each variable of such a private type. The difference to modules of class 2 is that here variables of the private types are declared in the client modules, whereas in class 2 modules the variable is itself hidden. Typical examples are the queue and stack types, and perhaps the most successful such data abstraction is the sequential file, also known as a *stream*.

This classification is not absolute. It cannot be, because all kinds share the common goal of hiding details. A module that shares aspects of classes 1 and 2 is the InOut used in previous examples: it hides the details of number representation and conversion as well as the two stream variables in and out. Nevertheless, we can formulate a few rules that serve as guidelines in the design of modules

1. Keep the number of imported identifiers small.

2. Rule 1 is particularly important for definition modules.

3. Export of variables should be considered as the exception, and imported variables should be treated as "read-only" objects.

We conclude this chapter with an example that essentially falls into category 3. Let our stated goal be the design of a *cross reference generator* for Modula programs. More precisely, the program's purpose is to read a text and to generate (1) a listing of the text with added line numbers and (2) a table of all encountered words (identifiers) in alphabetical order, each with a list of the numbers of the lines in which the word occurs. Moreover, comments and strings are to be skipped (i.e. their words are not to be listed), and Modula key symbols and standard identifiers are not to be listed either.

We quickly recognize the task as being divisible into the scanning of the source text (eliminating the parts that are to be skipped and ignored), and the recording and subsequent tabulating of the words. The first part is conveniently performed by the main program module, the latter by a subsidiary module which hides the data set and makes it accessible through two procedures: *Record* (i.e. include a word) and *Tabulate* (i.e. generate the requested table). A third module is used to generate the representation of numbers as sequences of decimal digits. The three principal modules involved are called XREF, TableHandler, and InOut.

We begin by presenting the main program XREF that scans the source text. A binary search is used to recognize key words. The data set is of the type *Table,* imported from the TableHandler in opaque mode.

```
DEFINITION MODULE TableHandler;
  EXPORT QUALIFIED
```

```modula2
      LineWidth, WordLength, Table, overflow,
      InitTable, Record, Tabulate;

    CONST LineWidth = 80; WordLength = 24;
    TYPE Table;
    VAR overflow: CARDINAL;  (* >0 means table full*)

    PROCEDURE InitTable(VAR t: Table);
    PROCEDURE Record(t: Table; VAR x: ARRAY OF CHAR; n: INTEGER);
      (*enter x,n in table t; string x must end with a blank*)
    PROCEDURE Tabulate(t: Table)
  END TableHandler.


  MODULE XREF;
    FROM InOut IMPORT
       Done, EOL, OpenInput, OpenOutput,
       Read, Write, WriteCard, WriteString, CloseInput, CloseOutput;
    FROM TableHandler IMPORT
       WordLength, Table, overflow, InitTable, Record, Tabulate;

    TYPE Alfa = ARRAY [0..9] OF CHAR;
    CONST N = 45;   (* No. of keywords *)
    VAR ch: CHAR;
     i,k,l,m,r,lno: CARDINAL;
     T: Table;
     id: ARRAY [0..WordLength-1] OF CHAR;
     key: ARRAY [1..N] OF Alfa;

    PROCEDURE copy;
    BEGIN Write(ch); Read(ch);
    END copy;

    PROCEDURE heading;
    BEGIN lno : = lno + 1; WriteCard(lno,5); Write(" ")
    END heading;

    BEGIN InitTable(T);
    key[ 1] : = "AND      ";      key[ 2] : = "ARRAY    ";      key[ 3] : = "BEGIN    ";
    key[ 4] : = "BITSET   ";      key[ 5] : = "BOOLEAN  ";      key[ 6] : = "BY       ";
    key[ 7] : = "CASE     ";      key[ 8] : = "CARDINAL ";      key[ 9] : = "CHAR     ";
    key[10] : = "CONST    ";      key[11] : = "DIV      ";      key[12] : = "DO       ";
    key[13] : = "ELSE     ";      key[14] : = "ELSIF    ";      key[15] : = "END      ";
    key[16] : = "EXIT     ";      key[17] : = "EXPORT   ";      key[18] : = "FALSE    ";
    key[19] : = "FOR      ";      key[20] : = "FROM     ";      key[21] : = "IF       ";
    key[22] : = "IMPORT   ";      key[23] : = "IN       ";      key[24] : = "INTEGER  ";
    key[25] : = "LOOP     ";      key[26] : = "MOD      ";      key[27] : = "MODULE   ";
    key[28] : = "NOT      ";      key[29] : = "OF       ";      key[30] : = "OR       ";
    key[31] : = "POINTER  ";      key[32] : = "PROCEDURE ";     key[33] : = "QUALIFIED ";
    key[34] : = "RECORD   ";      key[35] : = "REPEAT   ";      key[36] : = "RETURN   ";
    key[37] : = "SET      ";      key[38] : = "THEN     ";      key[39] : = "TO       ";
    key[40] : = "TRUE     ";      key[41] : = "TYPE     ";      key[42] : = "UNTIL    ";
```

```
key[43] := "VAR      ";        key[44] := "WHILE   ";        key[45] := "WITH    ";

OpenInput("MOD");
IF NOT Done THEN HALT END ;
OpenOutput("XREF");
lno := 0; Read(ch);
IF Done THEN heading;
 REPEAT
  IF (CAP(ch) >= "A") & (CAP(ch) <= "Z") THEN
   k := 0;
   REPEAT id[k] := ch; k := k + 1; copy
   UNTIL (ch < "0") OR
       (ch > "9") & (CAP(ch) < "A") OR
       (CAP(ch) > "Z");
   l := 1; r := N; id[k] := " ";
   REPEAT m := (l + r) DIV 2; i := 0; (*binary search*)
     WHILE (id[i] = key[m,i]) & (id[i] # " ") DO i := i + 1 END ;
    IF id[i] <= key[m,i] THEN r := m-1 END ;
    IF id[i] >= key[m,i] THEN l := m + 1 END ;
   UNTIL l > r;
   IF l = r + 1 THEN Record(T,id,lno) END
  ELSIF (ch >= "0") & (ch <= "9") THEN
   REPEAT copy
   UNTIL ((ch < "0") OR (ch > "9")) & ((ch < "A") OR (ch > "Z"))
  ELSIF ch = "(" THEN
   copy;
   IF ch = "*" THEN (*comment*)
    REPEAT
     REPEAT
      IF ch = EOL THEN
       copy; heading
      ELSE copy
      END
     UNTIL ch = "*";
     copy
    UNTIL ch = ")";
    copy
   END
  ELSIF ch = "'" THEN
   REPEAT copy UNTIL ch = "'";
   copy
  ELSIF ch = '"' THEN
   REPEAT copy UNTIL ch = '"';
   copy
  ELSIF ch = EOL THEN
   copy;
   IF Done THEN heading END
  ELSE copy
  END
 UNTIL NOT Done OR (overflow # 0)
END ;
```

```
IF overflow > 0 THEN
  WriteString("Table overflow"); WriteCard(overflow, 6);
  Write(EOL)
END ;
  Write(35C); Tabulate(T); CloseInput; CloseOutput
END XREF.
```

Next we present the table handler. As seen from its definition part, it exports the private type Table and its operations Record and Tabulate. Notably the structure of the tables, and thereby also the access and search algorithms remain hidden. The two most likely choices are the organizations of binary trees and of a hash table. Here we opt for the former choice. The example is therefore a further illustration of the use of pointers and dynamic data structures. The module contains a procedure to search and insert a tree element, and a procedure that traverses the tree for the required tabulation (see also the Chapter on dynamic data structures). Each tree node is a record with fields for the key, the left and right descendants, and (the head of) a list containing the line numbers.

```
IMPLEMENTATION MODULE TableHandler;
  FROM InOut IMPORT Write, WriteLn, WriteInt;
  FROM Storage IMPORT ALLOCATE;

  CONST TableLength = 3000;

  TYPE TreePtr = POINTER TO Word;
    ListPtr = POINTER TO Item;
    Item = RECORD num: INTEGER;
       next: ListPtr
      END ;
    Word = RECORD key: CARDINAL;   (*table index*)
        first: ListPtr;    (*list head*)
        left, right: TreePtr
      END ;
    Table = TreePtr;

  VAR id: ARRAY [0..WordLength] OF CHAR;
    ascinx: CARDINAL;
    asc: ARRAY [0..TableLength-1] OF CHAR;

  PROCEDURE InitTable(VAR t: Table);
  BEGIN NEW(t); t↑.right : = NIL
  END InitTable;

  PROCEDURE Search(p: TreePtr): TreePtr;
    (*search node with name equal to id*)
    TYPE Relation = (less, equal, greater);
    VAR q: TreePtr;
      r: Relation; i: CARDINAL;

    PROCEDURE rel(k: CARDINAL): Relation;
    (*compare id with asc[k]*)
      VAR i: CARDINAL;
```

```
      R: Relation; x,y: CHAR;
    BEGIN i : = 0; R : = equal;
      LOOP x : = id[i]; y : = asc[k];
        IF CAP(x) # CAP(y) THEN EXIT END ;
        IF x < = " " THEN RETURN R END ;
        IF x < y THEN R : = less ELSIF x > y THEN R : = greater
        END ;
        i : = i + 1; k : = k + 1
      END ;
      IF CAP(x) > CAP(y) THEN RETURN greater ELSE RETURN less
      END
    END rel;

  BEGIN q : = p↑.right; r : = greater;
    WHILE q # NIL DO
      p : = q; r : = rel(p↑.key);
      IF r = equal THEN RETURN p
      ELSIF r = less THEN q : = p↑.left
      ELSE q : = p↑.right
      END
    END ;
    NEW(q);   (*not found, hence insert*)
    IF q # NIL THEN
      WITH q↑ DO
        key : = ascinx; first : = NIL; left : = NIL; right : = NIL
      END ;
      IF r = less THEN p↑.left : = q ELSE p↑.right : = q END ;
      i : = 0;   (*copy identifier into asc table*)
      WHILE id[i] > " " DO
        IF ascinx = TableLength THEN
          asc[ascinx] : = " "; id[i] : = " "; overflow : = 1
        ELSE asc[ascinx] : = id[i]; ascinx : = ascinx + 1; i : = i + 1
        END
      END ;
      asc[ascinx] : = " "; ascinx : = ascinx + 1
    END ;
    RETURN q
  END Search;

  PROCEDURE Record(t: Table; VAR x: ARRAY OF CHAR; n: INTEGER);
    VAR p: TreePtr; q: ListPtr; i: CARDINAL;
  BEGIN i : = 0;
    REPEAT id[i] : = x[i]; i : = i + 1
    UNTIL (id[i-1] = " ") OR (i = WordLength);
    p : = Search(t);
    IF p = NIL THEN overflow : = 2 ELSE NEW(q);
      IF q = NIL THEN overflow : = 3 ELSE
        q↑.num : = n; q↑.next : = p↑.first; p↑.first : = q
      END
    END
  END Record;
```

```
PROCEDURE Tabulate(t: Table);

 PROCEDURE PrintItem(p: TreePtr);
  CONST L = 6;
    N = (LineWidth-WordLength) DIV L;
  VAR ch: CHAR;
    i,k: CARDINAL; q: ListPtr;
 BEGIN i : = WordLength + 1; k : = p↑.key;
  REPEAT ch : = asc[k];
   i : = i-1; k : = k + 1; Write(ch)
  UNTIL ch < = " ";
  WHILE i > 0 DO
   Write(" "); i : = i-1
  END ;
  q : = p↑.first; i : = N;
  WHILE q # NIL DO
   IF i = 0 THEN
    WriteLn; i : = WordLength + 1;
    REPEAT Write(" "); i : = i-1
    UNTIL i = 0;
    i : = N
   END ;
   WriteInt(q↑.num, L); q : = q↑.next; i : = i-1
  END ;
  WriteLn
 END PrintItem;

 PROCEDURE TraverseTree(p: TreePtr);
 BEGIN
  IF p # NIL THEN
   TraverseTree(p↑.left);
   PrintItem(p);
   TraverseTree(p↑.right)
  END
 END TraverseTree;

 BEGIN WriteLn; TraverseTree(t↑.right)
 END Tabulate;

BEGIN ascinx : = 0; id[WordLength] : = " "; overflow : = 0
END TableHandler.
```

26. Local modules

So far we have encountered modules as sections of text to be considered "side by side". However, we now have to learn that modules can be textually nested. An immediate consequence is that nested modules are not separately compilable. They are called *local modules,* and their only purpose is the hiding of details of their internally declared objects.

Each module establishes a *scope of visibility* of identifiers. This implies that objects declared in a scope (module) are visible only within that scope. Note that also procedures constitute a scope, and that the rules of visibility are essentially the same for procedures and modules. There is a difference, however, and it lies in two aspects:

1. For modules, the visibility range can be extended by listing an identifier in the module's export list. Then the identifier becomes visible also in the surrounding scope. This is not possible for procedures.

2. An identifier visible in the surrounding scope is also visible inside the local procedure. It is not visible inside a local module, unless the identifier is included in the module's import list.

The visibility rules of modules are illustrated by the following example:

```
VAR a,b: CARDINAL;
MODULE M;
  IMPORT a; EXPORT w, x;
  VAR u, v, w: CARDINAL;
  MODULE N;
    IMPORT u; EXPORT x,y;
    VAR x, y, z: CARDINAL;
        (* u, x, y, z visible here *)
  END N;
  (* a, u, v, w, x, y  visible here *)
END M;
(* a, b, w, x visible here *)
```

If an identifier is to cross several scope boundaries, it has to be listed in just as many import lists (or the module must be exported as a whole). Extending visibility from an inner module to the outside is achieved by export, extending from an outer scope to the inside by import. The rules are completely symmetric.

Now consider the following structure of modules N1, N2, and N3 nested in M:

```
MODULE M;
  VAR a: CARDINAL;

  MODULE N1;
    EXPORT b;
    VAR b: CARDINAL;
    (* only b visible here *)
```

```
        END N1;

        MODULE N2;
          EXPORT c;
          VAR c:  CARDINAL;
          (* only c visible here *)
        END N2;

        MODULE N3;
          IMPORT b, c;
          (* b, c visible here *)
        END N3
        (* a,b,c visible here *)
      END M
```

N3 imports an identifier from N2 and one from N1, identifiers which had been exported into their environment M. If we replace M by a "universe" (in which no local a could be declared), we recognize in this example the modules N1, N2, N3 as global modules discussed in the preceding chapter. In fact, all scope rules are identical for global and local modules. A global module, i.e. a compilation unit, could be said to be local to the universe.

Assume now that the variable c exported from N2 is also called b. This would result in a collision of names, because b is already known in M (exported from N1). This problem can be circumvented by applying qualified export, just as encountered for global modules. Now the b's belonging to N1 and N2 can be referenced (in M) as N1.b and N2.b respectively.

Qualified export is compulsory for global modules, because no designer of a global module knows whether or not his chosen identifier already exists in the universe. Qualified export is rather the exception for local modules, because a programmer knows its environment and therefore can chose identifiers such that name clashes are avoided.

A final remark is due concerning the differences of modules and procedures, which both establish a scope (nested in their environment). Whereas a module has no other role than that of providing a new scope, i.e. a visibility range, the procedure also establishes a new frame of existence for its local objects: they vanish upon termination of the procedure. In the case of a module, its local objects start to exist as soon as its outer frame of existence is created, and they continue to exist until that frame vanishes. However, the case of modules being local to a procedure is rare in practice (unless one also considers a main program to be not only a module, but also a procedure). The syntax of a local module is, like that of a program module, the following:

```
$   ModuleDeclaration = "MODULE" identifier [priority] ";"
$              {import}
$              [export]
$              block identifier.
$   priority = "[" ConstExpression "]".
```

(The purpose of indicating a priority will be discussed in the chapter on concurrency).

The following sample program demonstrates the use of a local module. The program's purpose is to read a text, check its conformity to EBNF syntax, and to generate a cross reference listing of the read text. The symbols are to be listed in two tables, one for terminal symbols, i.e. strings enclosed in quotes and identifiers written with capital letters only, and one for nonterminal symbols, i.e. other identifiers.

This specification suggests a subdivision similar to that of the XREF program in the preceding chapter. We further subdivide the task of scanning into reading individual EBNF symbols, the *lexical analysis* of text, and checking against the EBNF syntax rules, the *syntax analysis.* The program then consists of the main module called EBNF which imports both EBNFScanner (performing lexical analysis) and TableHandler (storing and tabulating the data). The latter is inherited from the previous chapter without alteration. All three modules further import InOut.

The main program operates according to the principle of top-down parsing like the example shown in the chapter on recursion. The difference is that the elements of text are not characters, but EBNF symbols, obtained one at a time by calling procedure GetSym of the scanner. Together with GetSym are imported its result variables sym, id, and lno. The identifier Id is assigned the character string denoting the symbol, if the symbol read was an identifier or a literal string. Note that sym is of type Symbol, which is also defined in the scanner module.

```
DEFINITION MODULE EBNFScanner;
 EXPORT QUALIFIED
   Symbol, sym, id, lno, GetSym, MarkError, SkipLine;

 TYPE Symbol = (ident, literal, lpar, lbk, lbr,
           bar, eql, period, rpar, rbk, rbr, other);

 CONST IdLength = 24;
 VAR sym: Symbol;     (*next symbol*)
  id: ARRAY [0..IdLength] OF CHAR;
  lno: CARDINAL;

 PROCEDURE GetSym;
 PROCEDURE MarkError(n: CARDINAL);
 PROCEDURE SkipLine;
END EBNFScanner.
```

This example illustrates again that knowledge of the imported definition module is both necessary and sufficient to construct the importing module.

```
MODULE EBNF;
 FROM InOut IMPORT
  Done, EOL, OpenInput, OpenOutput,
  Read, Write, WriteLn, WriteCard, WriteString, CloseInput, CloseOutput;
 FROM EBNFScanner IMPORT
  Symbol, sym, id, lno, GetSym, MarkError, SkipLine;
 FROM TableHandler IMPORT
  WordLength, Table, overflow, InitTable, Record, Tabulate;

 (*Syntax error codes:
   2 = ")" expected,  6 = identifier expected
   3 = "]" expected,  7 = " = " expected
   4 = "}" expected,  8 = "." expected
   5 = identifier, literal, "(", "[", or "{" expected *)

 VAR T0, T1: Table;
```

```
PROCEDURE skip(n: CARDINAL);
 (*skip until a symbol is found which starts an expression*)
BEGIN MarkError(n);
 WHILE (sym < lpar) OR (sym > period) DO GetSym END
END skip;

PROCEDURE Expression;

 PROCEDURE Term;

  PROCEDURE Factor;
  BEGIN
   IF sym = ident THEN
     Record(T0,id,lno); GetSym
   ELSIF sym = literal THEN
     Record(T1,id,lno); GetSym
   ELSIF sym = lpar THEN
    GetSym; Expression;
    IF sym = rpar THEN GetSym ELSE skip(2) END
   ELSIF sym = lbk THEN
    GetSym; Expression;
    IF sym = rbk THEN GetSym ELSE skip(3) END
   ELSIF sym = lbr THEN
    GetSym; Expression;
    IF sym = rbr THEN GetSym ELSE skip(4) END
   ELSE skip(5) END
  END Factor;

 BEGIN (*Term*) Factor;
  WHILE sym < bar DO Factor END
 END Term;

BEGIN (*Expression*) Term;
 WHILE sym = bar DO GetSym; Term END
END Expression;

PROCEDURE Production;
BEGIN (*sym = ident*)
 Record(T0,id,-INTEGER(lno)); GetSym;
 IF sym = eql THEN GetSym ELSE skip(7) END ;
 Expression;
 IF sym # period THEN MarkError(8); SkipLine END ;
 GetSym
END Production;

BEGIN (*Main*)
 OpenInput("EBNF");
 IF Done THEN
  OpenOutput("XREF"); InitTable(T0); InitTable(T1);
  GetSym;
```

```
      WHILE (sym = ident) & (overflow = 0) DO Production END ;
      IF overflow > 0 THEN
        WriteLn; WriteString("Table overflow");
        WriteCard(overflow, 6)
      END ;
      Write(35C); Tabulate(T0); Tabulate(T1);
      CloseInput; CloseOutput
    END
  END EBNF.
```

It is noteworthy that the requirement to list encountered symbols separated into terminals and nonterminals is mirrored by the fact that two variables of type Table are declared. The program's structure reflects that of the EBNF syntax. The reader is referred to the chapter defining EBNF.

The task of the scanner is to recognize individual symbols, to keep track of line numbers, and to generate a listing of the text read. An added complication arises from the fact that detected errors, i.e. disregard for EBNF syntax rules, need to be reported. The scanner keeps a record of the position of the last character read and, had an error been reported by a call of MarkError, inserts an error message line. This implies that an entire input line has to be read before its processing is begun, implying the necessity of a line buffer. These operations are line oriented, and are therefore encapsulated in a local module LineHandler.

```
  IMPLEMENTATION MODULE EBNFScanner;
   FROM InOut IMPORT EOL, Read, Write, WriteLn, WriteCard;

   VAR ch: CHAR;

   MODULE LineHandler;
    IMPORT EOL, ch, lno, Read, Write, WriteLn, WriteCard;
    EXPORT GetCh, MarkError, SkipLine;

    CONST LineWidth = 100;
    VAR cc: CARDINAL;    (*current character index*)
      cc1: CARDINAL;    (*character count limit*)
      cc2: CARDINAL;    (*character count on error line*)
      line: ARRAY [0..LineWidth-1] OF CHAR;

    PROCEDURE GetLine;   (*get next line*)
    BEGIN IF cc2 > 0 THEN
        WriteLn; cc2 := 0 (*error line*)
      END ;
     Read(ch);
     IF ch = 0C THEN  (*eof*)
      line[0] := 177C; cc1 := 1
     ELSE
      lno := lno + 1; WriteCard(lno, 5);
      Write(" "); cc1 := 0;
      LOOP
        Write(ch); line[cc1] := ch; cc1 := cc1 + 1;
        IF (ch = EOL) OR (ch = 0C) THEN EXIT END ;
```

```
      Read(ch)
    END
  END
END GetLine;

PROCEDURE GetCh;    (*get next character*)
BEGIN
 WHILE cc = cc1 DO
  cc : = 0; GetLine
 END ;
 ch : = line[cc]; cc : = cc + 1
END GetCh;

PROCEDURE MarkError(n: CARDINAL);
BEGIN IF cc2 = 0 THEN
    Write("*"); cc2 : = 3;
    REPEAT Write(" "); cc2 : = cc2 - 1
    UNTIL cc2 = 0
   END ;
 WHILE cc2 < cc DO
  Write(" "); cc2 : = cc2 + 1
 END ;
 Write("↑"); WriteCard(n,1); cc2 : = cc2 + 2
END MarkError;

PROCEDURE SkipLine;
BEGIN
 WHILE ch # EOL DO GetCh END ;
 GetCh
END SkipLine;

BEGIN cc : = 0; cc1 : = 0; cc2 : = 0
END LineHandler;

PROCEDURE GetSym;    (*get next symbol*)
 VAR i: CARDINAL;
BEGIN
 WHILE ch < = " " DO GetCh END ;
 IF ch = "/" THEN
  SkipLine;
  WHILE ch < = " " DO GetCh END
 END ;
 IF (CAP(ch) < = "Z") & (CAP(ch) > = "A") THEN
  i : = 0; sym : = literal;
  REPEAT
   IF i < IdLength THEN
    id[i] : = ch; i : = i + 1
   END ;
   IF ch > "Z" THEN sym : = ident END ;
   GetCh
  UNTIL (CAP(ch) < "A") OR (CAP(ch) > "Z");
```

```
      id[i] : = " "
    ELSIF ch = "'" THEN
     i : = 0; GetCh; sym : = literal;
     WHILE ch # "'" DO
      IF i < IdLength THEN
       id[i] : = ch; i : = i + 1
      END ;
      GetCh
     END ;
     GetCh; id[i] : = " "
    ELSIF ch = '"' THEN
     i : = 0; GetCh; sym : = literal;
     WHILE ch # '"' DO
      IF i < IdLength THEN
       id[i] : = ch; i : = i + 1
      END ;
      GetCh
     END ;
     GetCh; id[i] : = " "
    ELSIF ch = " = " THEN sym : = eql; GetCh
    ELSIF ch = "(" THEN sym : = lpar; GetCh
    ELSIF ch = ")" THEN sym : = rpar; GetCh
    ELSIF ch = "[" THEN sym : = lbk; GetCh
    ELSIF ch = "]" THEN sym : = rbk; GetCh
    ELSIF ch = "{" THEN sym : = lbr; GetCh
    ELSIF ch = "}" THEN sym : = rbr; GetCh
    ELSIF ch = "|" THEN sym : = bar; GetCh
    ELSIF ch = "." THEN sym : = period; GetCh
    ELSIF ch = 177C THEN sym : = other
    ELSE sym : = other; GetCh
    END
  END GetSym;

  BEGIN lno : = 0; ch : = " "
  END EBNFScanner.
```

The output of this program when applied to the syntax of Modula-2 is listed in the Appendix.

27. Sequential input and output

The usefulness and the success of high-level programming languages rests on the principle of abstractions, the hiding of details that pertain to the computer which is used to execute the program rather than to the algorithm expressed by the program. The domain that has most persistently resisted abstraction is that of input and output operations. This is not surprising, because input and output inherently involve the activation of devices that are peripheral to the computer, and whose structure, function, and operation differ strongly among various kinds and brands. Many programming languages have typically incorporated statements for reading and writing data in sequential form without reference to specific devices or storage media. Such an abstraction has many advantages, but there exist always applications where some property of some device is to be utilized that is poorly, if at all, available through the standard statements of the language. Also, generality is usually costly, and consequently operations that are conveniently implemented for some devices may be inefficient if applied to other devices. Hence, there also exists a genuine desire to make transparent the properties of some devices for applications that require their efficient utilization. Simplification and generalization by suppression of details is then in direct conflict with the desire for transparency for efficient use.

In Modula this intrinsic dilemma has been resolved - or rather circumvented - by not including any statements for input and output at all. This extreme approach was made acceptable because of two facilities. First, there exists the module structure allowing the construction of a hierarchy of (library) modules representing various levels of abstraction. Second, Modula permits the expression of computer specific operations, such as communication with peripheral interfaces. These operations are typically contained in modules at the lowest level of this hierarchy, and are therefore counted among the so-called *low-level facilities*. A program wishing to ignore the details of device handling imports procedures from the standard modules at the higher levels of this hierarchy. One desiring utmost efficiency or requiring access to specific properties of specific devices either uses low-level modules, so-called device drivers, or uses the primitives themselves. In the latter case, the programmer pays the price of intransportability, for his programs refer directly to particulars of either his computer or its operating system.

It is impossible to present in this context any operations of devices at the low levels of the module hierarchy, because there exists a wide variety of such devices. We restrict the following material to the presentation of the typical hierarchy of modules used in performing conventional input and output operations, and to the description of the standard module InOut already encountered in examples in preceding chapters. In addition, we postulate some operations that are to be available in every implementation of Modula, although we wish to specify rigidly neither the names of the module containing them nor the set of remaining operations included in such modules. We wish to emphasize again that the hierarchy of these Modules and their exports do not belong to the language proper, although it is recognized that any programming without their availability would be cumbersome.

We generally distinguish between legible and illegible input and output. Legible input and output serves to communicate between the computer and its user. Mostly its elements are characters i.e. data of type CHAR; the exception is graphical input and output. Legible data are input through keyboards, card readers, etc. Legible output is generated by displays and printers. Illegible input and output is made from and to so-called peripheral storage media, such as disks and tapes, but also from sensors - e.g. in laboratories or drawing offices - and to devices that are controlled by computers, such as plotters, factory assembly lines, traffic signals, and networks. Data for illegible input and output can be of any type, and need not be of type CHAR.

The vast majority of input and output operations of both the legible and illegible variety is appropriately considered as *sequential*. Their data are of a structure that does not exist as a basic data structuring method in Modula, such as the array or the record. Nevertheless we give it a name and call it a *stream*, whose characteristics are

1. All elements of a stream are of the same type, the stream's base type. If it is CHAR, the stream is called a *text stream*.

2. The number of elements of the stream is not known a priori. The stream is therefore (a simple case of) a dynamic structure. The number of elements is called the *length* of the stream, and the stream with length 0 is called the *empty stream*.

3. A stream can be modified only by appending elements at its end (or by deleting the entire stream). Appending an element is called *writing*.

4. Only a single element of a stream is visible (accessible) at any one time, namely the element at the stream's current *position*. Accessing this element is called *reading*. A read operation typically advances the stream's position to the next element.

5. A stream has a *mode* : it is either being written or read. Hence every stream has an associated state consisting of length, position, and mode.

In passing we state that the stream as described above is perhaps the most successful case of data abstraction encountered. It is certainly more widely used in actual practice than the often quoted examples of stacks and queues. The language Pascal has included it among its basic data structuring methods along with arrays, records, and sets. In Pascal, streams are called (sequential) files, and legible streams (which base type CHAR) are called textfiles.

Before proceeding with the postulation and explanation of a module hierarchy performing input and output, we wish to point out an important separation of function within IO operations. It concerns in particular the legible input and output. On the one hand, there is the actual transport of data to and from the computer. This involves the activation and sensing of the state of the peripheral device, be it a keyboard, a display, or a printer. On the other hand, there is the function of transforming the representation of data. If, for example, the value of an expression of type CARDINAL is to be transmitted to a display, the computer-internal representation must be transformed into the decimal representation as a sequence of digits. The display device then translates the character representation (usually consisting of 8 bits for each character) into a pattern of visible dots or lines. However, the former translation can be considered as device independent, and is therefore a prime candidate for separation from device specific operations. It can be performed by the same routines without regard whether the stream is to be stored on a disk or to be made visible on a display. This transformation is also called *formatting*.

A third class of functions that can well be separated pertain to devices associated with more than a single stream, the primary example being a disk store. We refer to the operations of allocating storage space and associating names with individual streams or files. Considering that streams (and files) are dynamic structures, storage allocation is of considerable complexity. The naming of individual files and in particular the management of directories to quickly locate individual files is another task requiring an elaborate mechanism. Both storage allocation and directory management are the tasks of a resident operating system. There seem to exist as many ways to manage these tasks as there exist operating systems. And this is precisely where diversity transcends the many levels of input and output operations, making it exceedingly difficult to postulate binding conventions for file handling primitives that are both operating system independent and efficiently implementable on many (or even only more than one) underlying operating system. Our solution is therefore to offer a hierarchy of modules, leaving the choice of entry level to the individual programmer. Entering at a high level brings the advantage of simplicity of concept and program portability (perhaps at the expense of efficiency); entering at a low level opens the full range of possibilities offered by the installed operating system at the expense of portability of programs. In the latter case, the programmer is strongly urged to confine the system dependent statements to a minimal number of places in his program.

The top of our module hierarchy is formed by the standard module InOut. It contains two text streams, one is the standard input source, the other the standard output stream. InOut offers the following facilities:

1. A set of procedures for reading data from the stream *in* serves to input formatted data. These procedures are

```
Read(ch)
ReadString(s)
ReadInt(x)
ReadCard(x)
```

The end of the stream is recognized by inspecting the exported variable Done. Its value is FALSE, if the preceding read operation was unsuccessful because the end had been reached. In this case, Read(ch) assigns the value 0C to ch. The typical program schema for sequential reading is therefore

```
Read(ch);
WHILE Done Do
  process(ch); Read(ch);
END
```

2. A set of procedures for writing data on stream *out* serves to output formatted data. These procedures are

```
Write(ch)
WriteString(s)
WriteLn
WriteInt(x,n)
WriteCard(x,n)
WriteOct(x,n)
WriteHex(x,n)
```

3. The procedures

```
OpenInput(s)
OpenOutput(s)
CloseInput
CloseOutput
```

serve to associate files with the standard streams in and out. Unless OpenInput is called, input data are presumed to originate from the standard input device, normally the operator's keyboard. Calling OpenInput causes the request of a file name from the standard input device, and the association of the stream in with the specified file. Similarly, output data are directed at the standard device, normally the operator's terminal, until OpenOutput is called, whereafter it is associated with a specified file. A call of CloseInput (CloseOutput) returns input (output) to the standard device. Opened files **must** be closed before the program terminates.

The module InOut effectively achieves independence from any underlying operating system through the stream abstraction and by hiding two standard streams, whose declaration may therefore include characteristics of the operating system for the sake of efficiency in lower level modules. Also, the module hides highly operating system dependent facilities such as naming, opening and closing files. It also allows the use of the same formatting procedures for IO with keyboard, display, and files. Further details can be gathered from the following definition of module InOut.

```
DEFINITION MODULE InOut;
  EXPORT QUALIFIED
    EOL, Done, termCH,
    OpenInput, OpenOutput, CloseInput, CloseOutput,
    Read, ReadString, ReadInt, ReadCard,
    Write, WriteLn, WriteString, WriteInt, WriteCard, WriteOct, WriteHex;

  CONST EOL = 36C;
  VAR Done:  BOOLEAN;
    termCH:  CHAR;

  PROCEDURE OpenInput(defext: ARRAY OF CHAR);
    (*request a file name and open input file "in".
     Done : = "file was successfully opened".
     If open, subsequent input is read from this file.
     If name ends with ".", append extension defext*)

  PROCEDURE OpenOutput(defext: ARRAY OF CHAR);
    (*request a file name and open output file "out"
     Done : = "file was successfully opened.
     If open, subsequent output is written on this file*)

  PROCEDURE CloseInput;
    (*closes input file; returns input to terminal*)

  PROCEDURE CloseOutput;
    (*closes output file; returns output to terminal*)

  PROCEDURE Read(VAR ch: CHAR);
    (*Done : = NOT in.eof*)

  PROCEDURE ReadString(VAR s: ARRAY OF CHAR);
    (*read string, i.e. sequence of characters not containing
     blanks nor control characters; leading blanks are ignored.
```

END InOut.

Input is terminated by any character <= " ";
this character is assigned to termCH.
DEL is used for backspacing when input from terminal*)

PROCEDURE ReadInt(VAR x: INTEGER);
  (*read string and convert to integer. Syntax:
   integer = ["+"|"-"] digit {digit}.
   Leading blanks are ignored.
   Done := "integer was read"*)

PROCEDURE ReadCard(VAR x: CARDINAL);
  (*read string and convert to cardinal. Syntax:
   cardinal = digit {digit}.
   Leading blanks are ignored.
   Done := "cardinal was read"*)

PROCEDURE Write(ch: CHAR);

PROCEDURE WriteLn;   (*terminate line*)

PROCEDURE WriteString(s: ARRAY OF CHAR);

PROCEDURE WriteInt(x: INTEGER; n: CARDINAL);
  (*write integer x with (at least) n characters on file "out".
   If n is greater than the number of digits needed,
   blanks are added preceding the number*)

PROCEDURE WriteCard(x,n: CARDINAL);
PROCEDURE WriteOct(x,n: CARDINAL);
PROCEDURE WriteHex(x,n: CARDINAL);
END InOut.

A further important detail is that InOut specifies the character constant EOL, denoting the end of a line. (Hence, Write(EOL) is equivalent to WriteLn). Notably, a line end is denoted by this single character.

Formatted input and output of real numbers is performed by the standard companion module *RealInOut*. It provides the procedures

    ReadReal(x)
    WriteReal(x,n),
    WriteRealOct(x,n)

and accesses streams via InOut's procedures Read and Write. Therefore redirection of input and output by calling OpenInput or OpenOutput also affects the operations of RealInOut.

    DEFINITION MODULE RealInOut;
    EXPORT QUALIFIED ReadReal, WriteReal, WriteRealOct, Done;

    VAR Done: BOOLEAN;

    PROCEDURE ReadReal(VAR x: REAL);

(∗Read REAL number x according to syntax:

[" + "|"-"] digit {digit} ["." digit {digit}]
["E"[" + "|"-"] digit [digit]]

Done : = "a number was read".
At most 7 digits are significant, leading zeroes not
counting. Maximum exponent is 38. Input terminates
with a blank or any control character. DEL is used
for backspacing∗)

PROCEDURE WriteReal(x: REAL; n: CARDINAL);
(∗Write x using n characters. If fewer than n characters
are needed, leading blanks are inserted∗)

PROCEDURE WriteRealOct(x: REAL);
(∗Write x in octal form with exponent and mantissa∗)

END RealInOut.

The module InOut contains a switch directing the data streams to either the terminal or the file system, depending on whether a file had been opened. On the level below InOut we therefore find two modules, one for input and output from and to the terminal, the other representing the file system. Both shall be described here, because in many cases a programmer will want to access them directly.

For terminal input/output we postulate the module *Terminal.* It exports a procedure Read for reading data from the keyboard, and a procedure Write for writing on the screen (or the terminal's typewriter).

DEFINITION MODULE Terminal;
EXPORT QUALIFIED
Read, BusyRead, ReadAgain,
Write, WriteLn, WriteString;

PROCEDURE Read(VAR ch: CHAR);
PROCEDURE BusyRead(VAR ch: CHAR); (∗returns 0C, if no character was typed∗)
PROCEDURE ReadAgain; (∗causes the last character read to be returned again
upon the next call of Read∗)
PROCEDURE Write(ch: CHAR);
PROCEDURE WriteLn; (∗terminate line∗)
PROCEDURE WriteString(s: ARRAY OF CHAR);
END Terminal.

The next lower level of the module hierarchy connecting InOut with a computer's *file system* embodies the concept of the stream. With due consideration to this level's proximity to actual file systems, we refrain from postulating a binding definition for all possible implementations. Even the name of this module may differ among various installations. However, a number of declarations is postulated that the programmer may assume to be available in all implemented Modula systems. These will be listed below, but first we turn our attention to the concept of streams, i.e. the structure of sequences.

We distinguish between two kinds of streams, namely *text streams* with base type CHAR, and *word streams* with base type WORD. The latter type is dependent on the underlying computer systems, but in any case is compatible for parameter passing with all types that are allocated exactly one word of memory, such as INTEGER, CARDINAL, and BITSET. (For details, refer to the subsequent chapter on low-level facilities).

This module exports a type denoting a stream. Here we shall appropriately call this type STREAM, but allow for deviation recognizing that in some implementations this type may be identical to a given type exported from the underlying file system. This arrangement is actually to be preferred, because a stream is ultimately implemented as a file; what turns the file into a stream is merely the restriction of the set of applied operations to those of sequential reading and writing. These operations are, if s is of type STREAM

ReadChar(s,ch)   Read Word(s,w)
WriteChar(s,ch)   WriteWord(s,w)

The module also exports a facility to define and to examine a stream's mode, in particular whether or not its end had been reached upon reading. If the module streams is not directly included in the file system, then it exports a procedure to associate (connect) a new stream with a file (which is obtained from the file system), and to disconnect the stream from the file, when the stream is no longer needed.

As an example of such a module we present its definition part as implemented for the RT-11 operating system of PDP-11 computers. This module, called *Streams,* imports a type FILE from a module *Files.* This module actually interfaces Modula programs with the RT-11 operating system, which identifies files by cardinal numbers, the so-called channel numbers. The procedure Connect associates an RT-11 file, i.e. an object of type FILE, with a stream, i.e. an object of type STREAM, and determines whether it is to be a character or a word stream.

```
DEFINITION MODULE Streams; (*for RT-11*)
 FROM SYSTEM IMPORT WORD;
 FROM Files IMPORT FILE;

 EXPORT QUALIFIED
  STREAM, Connect, Disconnect,
  WriteWord, WriteChar, EndWrite,
  ReadWord, ReadChar, EOS,
  Reset, SetPos, GetPos;

 TYPE STREAM;

 PROCEDURE Connect(VAR s: STREAM; f: FILE; ws: BOOLEAN);
  (*connect stream s with open file f.
   f is RT11 channel number.
   ws = "s is a word stream, not a character stream" *)
 PROCEDURE Disconnect(VAR s: STREAM; closefile: BOOLEAN);
 PROCEDURE WriteWord(s: STREAM; w: WORD);
 PROCEDURE WriteChar(s: STREAM; ch: CHAR);
 PROCEDURE EndWrite(s: STREAM);
 PROCEDURE ReadWord(s: STREAM; VAR w: WORD);
```

```
        PROCEDURE ReadChar(s: STREAM; VAR ch: CHAR);
        PROCEDURE EOS(s: STREAM): BOOLEAN;
        PROCEDURE Reset(s: STREAM);
        PROCEDURE SetPos(s: STREAM; high, low: CARDINAL);
        PROCEDURE GetPos(s: STREAM; VAR high, low: CARDINAL);
     END Streams.
```

In the case of text streams, the procedures ReadChar and WriteChar perform the necessary transformations of the representation of line ends. In Modula, a line end is represented by the single character EOL, in RT-11 files by the character pair cr, lf (15C, 12C). If the end of a stream had been reached, ReadChar(s,ch) assigns the value 0C to ch.

A programmer wishing to make use of further file operations made available by the operating system needs to access these operations directly by importing them from the module Files. For his benefit, its definition part is specified below. Of particular interest are the procedures Lookup, Create, and Close. They are needed by all programs using Streams, because an RT-11 file needs either to be looked up in RT-11's file directory or to be created before a stream can be connected with it. Note that an RT-11 file name consists of exactly 12 characters, the first three designating the medium, the next six being the actual file identifier, and the last three forming the so-called *name extension*.

```
     DEFINITION MODULE Files;     (*Ch. Jacobi, for RT-11*)

     FROM SYSTEM IMPORT  ADDRESS, WORD;

     EXPORT QUALIFIED FILE, FileName, Lookup, Create, Delete,
              Release, Close, WriteBlock, ReadBlock, Rename;

     TYPE FILE = [0..15];
        FileName = ARRAY [0..11] OF CHAR;

     PROCEDURE Lookup(f: FILE; fn: FileName; VAR reply: INTEGER);
        (* lookup file f in dictionnary
          reply: >= 0 = done, file length
              < 0 = error: -1 = channel used, -2 = file not found *)

     PROCEDURE Create(f: FILE; fn: FileName; VAR reply: INTEGER);
        (* create a new file f; no entry in dictionnary.
          reply: >= 0 = done, file length
              < 0 = error: -1 = channel used, -2 = no space *)

     PROCEDURE Delete(f: FILE; fn: FileName; VAR reply: INTEGER);
        (* delete file f and its entry from dictionnary.
          reply: >= 0 = done, file length
              < 0 = error: -1 = channel used, -2 = file not found *)

     PROCEDURE Close(f: FILE);
        (* close file f and record it in dictionnary *)

     PROCEDURE Release(f: FILE);
        (* release file f, no entry in dictionnary *)
```

```
    PROCEDURE ReadBlock(f: FILE; p: ADDRESS; blknr, wcount: CARDINAL;
                VAR reply: INTEGER);
     (* read from file f
       p:     address of buffer
       blknr: blocknumber of first block to read
       wcount: number of words to read
       reply: >= 0 = number of words transferred
           < 0 = error: -1 = hard error, -2 = channel not open *)

    PROCEDURE WriteBlock(f: FILE; p: ADDRESS; blknr, wcount: CARDINAL;
                VAR reply: INTEGER);
     (* write to file f
       p:     address of buffer
       blknr: blocknumber of first block to write
       wcount: number of words to write
       reply: >= 0 = number of words transferred
           < 0 = error: -1 = hard error, -2 = channel not open *)

    PROCEDURE Rename(f: FILE; new, old: FileName;
                VAR reply: INTEGER);
     (* renames file f which must not be open
       reply: 0 = done
           < 0 = error: -1 = channel used, -2 = file not found; *)
    END Files.
```

We conclude the presentation of file handling under RT-11 by noting the following hierarchy of modules:

```
        InOut --> Streams --> Files --> RT11.
```

Hence, a call of, for example, Read in InOut implies a call of ReadChar in Streams, which may cause a call of ReadBlock in Files, which implies a call of an RT-11 primitive for reading a disk sector. As an example, we show the sequential processing of a file DATA.IN as a word stream into a file DATA.OUT as a character stream under RT-11.

```
    FROM Files IMPORT FILE, Lookup, Create, Close;
    FROM Streams IMPORT
        STREAM, Connect, ReadWord, WriteChar, EOS, Disconnect;

    VAR f1, f2: FILE;
      s1, s2: STREAM
      x: CARDINAL; y: CHAR; reply: INTEGER;

    BEGIN f1 := 1; f2 := 2; (*RT11 channel numbers*)
      Lookup(f1, "DK DATA IN ", reply);
      Create(f2, "DK DATA OUT", reply);
      Connect(s1, f1, TRUE); Connect(s2, f2, FALSE);
      ReadWord(s1,x);
      WHILE NOT EOS(s1) DO
        process(x,y); WriteChar(s2,y); ReadWord(s1,x)
      END;
```

```
        Disconnect(s1, FALSE);  Disconnect(s2, TRUE);
      END
```

An example of an implementation which merges the level Streams with the level Files, i.e.
presents a file system that properly includes the abstraction of streams, is the Medos system
for the Lilith computer. We present the relevant part of its definition module and then list
the program part that performs the same task of sequential file processing shown above.

```
      DEFINITION MODULE FileSystem;  (*S.E.Knudsen, for Lilith*)
       FROM SYSTEM IMPORT  ADDRESS, WORD;
       EXPORT QUALIFIED
        File, Response,

        Create, Close, Lookup, Rename,
        SetRead, SetWrite, SetModify, SetOpen,
        Doio, SetPos, GetPos, Length,

        Reset, Again,
        ReadWord, WriteWord, ReadChar, WriteChar,

        Command, Flag, FlagSet;

      TYPE
      Response    = (done, notdone, notsupported, callerror,
                unknownmedium, unknownfile, paramerror,
                toomanyfiles, eom, deviceoff,
                softparityerror, softprotected, softerror,
                hardparityerror, hardprotected, timeout, harderror);
      Command     = (create, open, close, lookup, rename,
                setread, setwrite, setmodify, setopen,
                doio, setpos, getpos, length,
                setprotect, getprotect, setpermanent, getpermanent,
                getinternal);
      Flag     = (er, ef, rd, wr, ag, bytemode);
      FlagSet    = SET OF Flag;

      File     = RECORD res: Response;
                bufa, ela, ina, topa: ADDRESS;
                elodd, inodd, eof: BOOLEAN;
                flags: FlagSet;
                CASE com: Command OF
                  create, open, getinternal:  fileno, versionno: CARDINAL |
                  lookup:  new: BOOLEAN |
                  setpos, getpos, length:  highpos, lowpos: CARDINAL |
                  setprotect, getprotect:  wrprotect: BOOLEAN |
                  setpermanent, getpermanent:  on: BOOLEAN
                END;
               END;
```

(* The routines defined by the file system can be grouped in routines for
  1. Opening, closing and renaming of files.
     (Create, Close, Lookup, Rename)
  2. Reading and writing of files.
     (SetRead, SetWrite, SetModify, SetOpen, Doio)
  3. Positioning of files.
     (SetPos, GetPos, Length)
  4. Streamlike handling of files.
     (Reset, Again, ReadWord, WriteWord, ReadChar, WriteChar) *)

PROCEDURE Create(VAR f: File; mediumname: ARRAY OF CHAR);
  (* creates a new temporary (or nameless) file f on the named device. *)

PROCEDURE Close(VAR f: File);
  (* terminates the operations on file f, i.e. cuts off the
     connection between variable f and the file system. A temporary
     file will hereby be destroyed whereas a file with
     a not empty name remains in the directory for later use. *)

PROCEDURE Lookup(VAR f: File; filename: ARRAY OF CHAR; new: BOOLEAN);
  (* searches file 'filename'. If the file does not exist and 'new' is TRUE,
     a new file with the given name will be created. *)

PROCEDURE Rename(VAR f: File; filename: ARRAY OF CHAR);
  (* changes the name of the file to 'filename'. If the new
     name is empty, f is changed to be a temporary file. *)

PROCEDURE SetRead(VAR f: File);
  (* initializes the file for reading. *)

PROCEDURE SetWrite(VAR f: File);
  (* initializes the file for writing. *)

PROCEDURE SetModify(VAR f: File);
  (* initializes the file for modifying. *)

PROCEDURE SetOpen(VAR f: File);
  (* terminates any input- or output operations on the file. *)

PROCEDURE Doio(VAR f: File);
  (* is used in connection with SetRead, SetWrite and
     SetModify in order to read, write or modify a file
     sequentially. *)

PROCEDURE SetPos(VAR f: File; highpos, lowpos: CARDINAL);
  (* sets the current position of file f to byte
     highpos * 2**16 + lowpos. *)

PROCEDURE GetPos(VAR f: File; VAR highpos, lowpos: CARDINAL);
  (* returns the current byte position of file f. *)

```
PROCEDURE Length(VAR f: File; VAR highpos, lowpos: CARDINAL);
  (* returns the length of file f in highpos and lowpos. *)

PROCEDURE Reset(VAR f: File);
  (* sets the file into state opened and the position
     to the beginning of the file. *)

PROCEDURE Again(VAR f: File);
  (* prevents a subsequent call of ReadWord (or ReadChar)
     from reading the next value on the file. Instead, the
     value read just before the call of Again is returned
     once more. *)

PROCEDURE ReadWord(VAR f: File; VAR w: WORD);
  (* reads the next word on the file. *)

PROCEDURE WriteWord(VAR f: File; w: WORD);
  (* appends word w to the file. *)

PROCEDURE ReadChar(VAR f: File; VAR ch: CHAR);
  (* reads the next character on the file. *)

PROCEDURE WriteChar(VAR f: File; ch: CHAR);
  (* appends character ch to the file. *)

END FileSystem.
```

The example of file processing given previously using Streams now simplifies to the following program:

```
FROM FileSystem IMPORT
  File, Lookup, ReadWord, WriteChar, Close;

VAR f1, f2 : File;
  x: CARDINAL; y: CHAR;

BEGIN
  Lookup(f1, "DK.DATA.IN", FALSE);
  Lookup(f2, "DK.DATA.OUT", TRUE);
  ReadWord(f1,x);
  WHILE NOT f1.eof DO
    process(x,y); WriteChar(f2,y); ReadWord(f1,x)
  END;
  Close(f1); Close(f2)
END
```

The careful programmer will, of course, include tests for successful file lookups. In such details the various implementations differ, as is to be expected. In the RT-11 example, successful lookup is tested by inspecting the reply parameter of procedure Lookup; in the Medos example it is done by inspecting the res field of the file variable (which has a record structure). Specifically, the test is "fl.res = done", where done is a constant of the enumeration type Response exported by the module FileSystem. The careful programmer must also be aware of another subtle difference between the two versions: Whereas Create (for RT11) opens a new file unconditionally, Lookup (in Medos) creates a new file only if the third parameter is TRUE and no file already exists with the specified name. The field f2.new allows to detect whether or not f2 is indeed a new file. Otherwise the old file may be overwritten.

28. Screen-oriented input and output

Sequential input and output implies that elements of data can be transmitted without explicit indication of position. This is *natural,* if the position is predetermined by the storage medium, such as a tape (which by definition constitutes a sequence), or a keyboard (from which data originate in strict sequence in time), or a typewriter (where character positions are determined by the mechanical movement of the printing device). Even if the storage device would allow for greater flexibility, sequential input and output is *convenient,* if the structure of the data is inherently sequential. For example, a text is inherently sequential, and the omission of positioning information for each character is a great simplification of the reading and writing tasks. And lastly, sequential input and output is *economical,* because buffering of data is easily possible between processes (devices) that operate concurrently. All this explains, why sequential data handling is so common and highly recommendable.

However, there are applications which require the non-sequential treatment of data. Characteristically, each element then carries positioning information. For example, disk stores permit the selective reading and writing of individual blocks of data, so-called sectors. Often large sets of data are written in sequential fashion, but read selectively in parts. (These possibilities are indicated by the modules Files and FileSystem in the preceding chapter.)

Recently, non-sequential output has gained in significance because of the growing predominance of visual output media, i.e. displays which present the data on a screen. Most diplay terminals still operate in sequential mode, simply because the data are mostly text, but also because its sequential handling is conventional and many users are unaware of the advantages that can be gained from a non-sequential treatment.

We recognize two primary motivations for the use of non-sequential output:

1. The data include elements without inherent, natural sequentiality, such as lines, tables, figures, or pictures, i.e. so-called *graphics.*

2. The screen is to be used to display *several* sequences of output data independently and concurrently, i.e. the screen is used to simulate several displays, each carrying its own positioning information relative to the full screen.

We subsequently present two modules which specifically address these points. Because non-sequential operations offer much more flexibility, they cater to a much larger variety of applications. Hence, this subject is much less amenable to standardization. The modules presented subsequently are therefore to be understood as suggestions rather than as "final solutions". Nevertheless, they have proved to be highly useful and convenient in many practical applications.

An important subset of general graphics are *line drawings,* i.e. drawings that contain lines only. If augmented by text (short strings for captions etc.), line drawings are adequate in very many cases, such as diagrams and tables. For these applications we offer the module *LineDrawing.* It presumes the availability of a rectangular screen area and exports its width and height given in units of horizontal and vertical coordinates. The screen is presumed to be a matrix of dots called a *raster*. Each dot (raster element) can be accessed; here we assume that it can be painted white or black. The extension of this concept to multi-valued dots for either grey-tones or color is conceptually straight-forward.

The most important procedures contained in the module LineDrawing are called dot and area:

dot(c,x,y)

paints the raster element at coordinates x,y in "color" c, where c = 0 shall mean white and c = 1 black. Of course x,y are to lie within the screen area, i.e. 0 <= x < width, 0 <= y < height. We assume that the coordinate 0,0 denotes the lower left corner of the rectangular screen area.

area(c,x,y,w,h)

paints the rectangle with lower left corner at coordinate x,y and with width w and height h in "color" c. We may assume c = 0 to mean white, c = 1 light grey, c = 2 dark grey, c = 3 black; however, other implementations may offer a wider set of values or even real colors. Also, the technique of representing grey scales is left up to individual implementations. For example, the value c may directly control the intensity of the crt beam, or it may be used to select a dot pattern replicated over the specified rectangle. The use of this procedure is demonstrated in the module Queens given in the previous chapter on procedures.

```
DEFINITION MODULE LineDrawing;
 EXPORT QUALIFIED
  width, height, CharWidth, CharHeight, PaintMode,
  Px, Py, mode,
  dot, line, area, copyArea, clear, Write, WriteString;

TYPE PaintMode = (replace, add, invert, erase);

VAR Px, Py: INTEGER;  (*current coordinates of line drawing pen*)
   mode:  PaintMode; (*current mode for paint and copy*)
   width: INTEGER;  (*width of picture area, read-only*)
   height: INTEGER;  (*height of picture area, read-only*)
   CharWidth: INTEGER;  (*width of a character*)
   CharHeight: INTEGER;  (*height of a character*)

PROCEDURE dot(c: CARDINAL; x,y: INTEGER);
 (*place dot at coordinate x,y*)

PROCEDURE line(d,n: CARDINAL);
 (*draw a line of length n in direction d (angle = 45*d degrees) *)

PROCEDURE area(c: CARDINAL; x,y,w,h: INTEGER);
 (*paint the rectangular area at x,y of width w and height h in color c
  0 = white, 1 = light grey, 2 = dark grey, 3 = black*)

PROCEDURE copyArea(sx,sy,dx,dy,dw,dh: INTEGER);
 (*copy rectangular area at sx,sy into rectangle at dx,dy of
  width dw and height dh *)
```

PROCEDURE clear; (*clear the screen*)

PROCEDURE Write(ch: CHAR); (*write ch at pen's position*)

PROCEDURE WriteString(s: ARRAY OF CHAR);

END LineDrawing.

The procedure line manifests that even for graphics the sequential mode is sometimes highly desirable because of its convenience. In using this procedure, we assume the existence of an imagined pen which draws straight lines. This pen has, of course, an implied position. A call of

line(d,n)

moves the pen in direction d by n raster units. Hence, a sequence of calls produces a sequence of consecutive line segments without the necessity to indicate intermediate pen positions. In our proposal, we allow a few specific directions only, namely those with angles d*45 degrees for d = 0, 1, ... 7, d = 0 meaning a move in the positive x direction, i.e. to the right. This mode of drawing lines is sometimes called *turtle graphics*.

The pen's position is specified by the exported variables Px and Py. They are used in order to define the beginning of the first line segment and to reposition the pen for drawing other sequences of segments. The use of the turtle graphics technique with this module is shown by the following sample program. It draws a space filling curve invented by the mathematician Sierpinski, and it is also a fine example of the use of recursive procedures to generate a recursively defined pattern.

```
MODULE Sierpinski;
  FROM Terminal IMPORT Read;
  FROM LineDrawing IMPORT width, height, Px, Py, clear, line;

  CONST SquareSize = 512;

  VAR i,h,x0,y0: CARDINAL; ch: CHAR;

  PROCEDURE A(k: CARDINAL);
  BEGIN
   IF k > 0 THEN
     A(k-1); line(7, h); B(k-1); line(0, 2*h);
     D(k-1); line(1, h); A(k-1)
   END
  END A;

  PROCEDURE B(k: CARDINAL);
  BEGIN
   IF k > 0 THEN
     B(k-1); line(5, h); C(k-1); line(6, 2*h);
     A(k-1); line(7, h); B(k-1)
   END
  END B;
```

```
PROCEDURE C(k: CARDINAL);
BEGIN
 IF k > 0 THEN
   C(k-1); line(3, h); D(k-1); line(4, 2*h);
   B(k-1); line(5, h); C(k-1)
 END
END C;

PROCEDURE D(k: CARDINAL);
BEGIN
 IF k > 0 THEN
   D(k-1); line(1, h); A(k-1); line(2, 2*h);
   C(k-1); line(3, h); D(k-1)
 END
END D;

BEGIN clear; i : = 0; h : = SquareSize DIV 4;;
 x0 : = CARDINAL(width) DIV 2; y0 : = CARDINAL(height) DIV 2 + h;
 REPEAT i : = i + 1; x0 : = x0-h;
  h : = h DIV 2; y0 : = y0 + h; Px : = x0; Py : = y0;
  A(i); line(7,h); B(i); line(5,h);
  C(i); line(3,h); D(i); line(1,h); Read(ch)
 UNTIL (i = 6) OR (ch = 33C);
 clear
END Sierpinski.
```

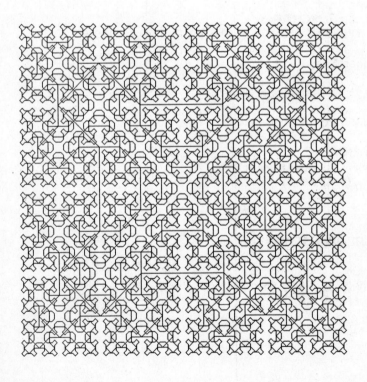

LineDrawing offers procedures for drawing lines and rectangular patterns. More complicated figures can be drawn by painting individual dots with calls of the procedure dot. A relatively important geometric element is the circle. We therefore present a procedure for drawing circles with center coordinates x,y and radius r. The interesting feature of this method is that it avoids the use of numbers of type REAL, and is therefore relatively efficient.

The equation of a circle is $x\uparrow2 + y\uparrow2 = r\uparrow2$. After drawing a dot at position x,y we wish to compute the coordinates of the next dot, namely $x+dx$ and $y+dy$. The ratio dy/dx is given by the first derivative of the equation above, and it is -x/y. Hence we can specify $dx = -k*y$ and $dy = k*y$, where k is a sufficiently small constant determining the coarsity of the circle that is approximated by a sequence of polygon segments. Restricting ourselves to the use of fixed-point fractions represented as scaled integers, we use $c1 = 1/k$ and compute the next values of x and y as

    x := x - y DIV c1; y := y + x DIV c1

Assuming the availability of a screen with a width and height of (at least) 512 points, we require 9 bits for the representation of coordinates. Assuming furthermore a computer with a wordsize of 16 bits, 7 bits are left for the fractional part, i.e. we can think of our integer coordinates as having a binary point 7 bits from the right, and we obtain the truncated whole part of x by dividing it by $c2 = 2\uparrow7 = 200B$. The constant c1 is chosen as large as possible such that, for the largest values of x and y the computed increments become unity.

```
        PROCEDURE DrawCircle(x0,y0,r: INTEGER);
          CONST c1 = 400B; c2 = 200B;
          VAR x,y: INTEGER;
        BEGIN
          r := r*c2; x := r; y := 0; r := r-1;
          REPEAT dot(1, x DIV c2 + x0, y DIV c2 + y0);
            x := x - y DIV c1; y := y + x DIV c1
          UNTIL (x >= r) & (y <= 0)
        END DrawCircle
```

Note: This algorithm is actually more subtle than may appear and the verification of its proper functioning requires some careful numeric analysis of truncation effects.

A tool for drawing graphic elements gains significantly in usefulness when it is coupled with an appropriate input device. Let us presume the existence of some input device that allows to sense movements on a plane. From this device we can read its position in terms of x and y coordinates. Furthermore, we presume that a small set of keys is associated with this device, whose states can also be sensed.

We call this input device a *Mouse,* a name that is a reflection of a particular realization of the given specifications as a device that is hand-held and moved around on the table. The fact that it is equipped with three keys (eyes) and is connected to the keyboard by a thin, perhaps grey, cable has given this device its name.

The mouse's position is made visible on the screen by a mark, called the *cursor.* It is thereby brought in relation to the screen and to the position of individual objects drawn on the screen. The technique of drawing a cursor and relating its position on the screen to the mouse's movements on the table remains hidden inside a module which shall be called *Mouse.* The user does not have to be aware of its details, nor even of whether it is based on hardware facilities or implemented in software. Its essential property is, however, that the cursor can be positioned at each raster element, thereby giving the input device the highest useful resolution.

The procedures used for operating the Mouse are *TrackMouse* and *FlipCursor*. TrackMouse is used to track the movements of the mouse, i.e. the user's hand. It reads the Mouse's position and draws the cursor accordingly, assigning its coordinates to the exported variables Mx and My. Usually, TrackMouse is called within a tight loop until a key is depressed signalling that some action related to the indicated coordinates is requested. The procedure FlipCursor activates a toggle switch turning the cursor on and off. Its existence is important, if the cursor is to be temporarily removed from the screen. For example, the author's implementation of Mouse on the Lilith computer requires that the cursor be off while elements are drawn or written (or erased). The current value of the toggle switch is represented by the exported variable curOn.

The procedure ShowMenu allows for a convenient manner to input commands. Its call causes a set of command words, given by a text parameter, to be displayed at the current position of the cursor. This display is to be understood as a *menu* of currently available commands. By subsequent movements of the Mouse one of the commands may be selected. ShowMenu is supposed to be called when a specific Mouse key is depressed. As soon as that key is released, control is returned with the parameter selection indicating the command word selected at that moment. The use of this menu is a powerful technique for flexible command input with the need for a single, simple input device only which at the same time is used to indicate the position of the object to which the command applies. The command menu appears at the place of the cursor, i.e. where the operator has currently focussed his attention.

```
DEFINITION MODULE Mouse;
 EXPORT QUALIFIED keys, Mx, My, curOn, mode,
    TrackMouse, FlipCursor, ShowMenu;

 VAR keys:  BITSET;   (*Mouse keys*)
   Mx, My: INTEGER;   (*Mouse and cursor coordinates*)
   curOn: BOOLEAN;  (*cursor toggle switch; initial value = FALSE*)
   mode:  CARDINAL;

 PROCEDURE TrackMouse;
  (*read Mouse coordinates Mx, My, and keys;
   move cursor accordingly*)

 PROCEDURE FlipCursor;
  (*toggle switch for cursor*)

 PROCEDURE ShowMenu(text: ARRAY OF CHAR; VAR selection: INTEGER);
   (*show menu text at current cursor position, then follow the Mouse's
    movements for command selection until menu key is released.
    Selection = 0 means that no command was selected. In the text, command
    lines are separated by "|". Command words have at most 7 characters,
    and there must be at most 8 commands *)
 END Mouse.
```

A use of the module LineDrawing together with Mouse is demonstrated by the following program *Draw*. It allows to draw pictures on a square area consisting of a raster with 64*64 "dots". Each "dot" is represented by a square area of 8∗8 raster dots. Using the menu technique, different colors or shades can be selected for painting. There are many ways in which this program can be extended or embellished. Its principal structure is

```
initialize screen;
FlipCursor; (∗on∗)
REPEAT TrackCursor;
  IF (a key is depressed) & (Mouse has moved) THEN
    FlipCursor; (∗off∗)
    perform requested action;
    FlipCursor; (∗on∗)
  END;
  BusyRead(ch);
  (∗interpret typed character∗)
UNTIL ch = ESC;
clear screen
```

The example also shows how input can "simultaneously" be read from the Mouse keys and the keyboard (usually used for text input only, but occasionally to signal actions). Keyboard input is obtained through the procedure BusyRead which, in contrast to the conventional Read, does not wait for the next keystroke, but instead immediately returns the value 0C, if no character is present.

```
MODULE Draw;
 FROM Terminal IMPORT BusyRead;
 FROM LineDrawing IMPORT
   width, height, Px, Py, dot, line, area, clear;
 FROM Mouse IMPORT
   keys, Mx, My, FlipCursor, TrackMouse, ShowMenu;

 CONST L = 512; (*SquareSize*)
   ESC = 33C; DEL = 177C;

 VAR i, color, x0, y0, x1, y1: INTEGER;
   minx, maxx, miny, maxy: INTEGER;
   ch: CHAR;

 PROCEDURE SetScreen;
 BEGIN area(1,0,0,width,height);
   Px : = minx; Py : = miny; area(0,Px,Py,L,L);
   line(0,L); line(2,L); line(4,L); line(6,L)
 END SetScreen;

BEGIN
 minx : = (width-L) DIV 2; miny : = (height-L) DIV 2;
 maxx : = minx + L; maxy : = miny + L; color : = 3;
 SetScreen; FlipCursor; (*switch cursor on*)
 REPEAT TrackMouse;
  IF 14 IN keys THEN
    ShowMenu("white|grey0|grey1|black", i);
    IF i # 0 THEN color : = i-1 END
  ELSIF (15 IN keys) & (minx < = Mx) & (Mx < maxx)
     & (miny < = My) & (My < maxy) THEN
   x1 : = (Mx - minx) DIV 8; y1 : = (My - miny) DIV 8;
   IF (x1 # x0) OR (y1 # y0) THEN
    FlipCursor; (*off*)
    area(color, minx + x1*8, miny + y1*8, 8, 8);
    x0 : = x1; y0 : = y1;
    FlipCursor (*on*)
   END
  END ;
  BusyRead(ch);
  IF ch = DEL THEN
    FlipCursor; SetScreen; FlipCursor
  END
 UNTIL ch = ESC;
 clear
END Draw.
```

We now turn our attention to a module that permits to simulate the availability of *several displays* on a single screen. Each simulated display is represented by a rectangle in which output operations for graphics and for text are available as if the rectangle represented a full screen. Such a rectangular area is called a *window,* because it may be considered as a window through which a selected part of a document may be viewed. An application of this technique was used for the postfix conversion program in the previous chapter on procedures.

Using the module called *WindowHandler,* windows can be opened (created) and closed upon demand. Each window is displayed as a rectangular area carrying a title, which is specified when the window is opened. Windows can be moved, as if they were pieces of paper lying on a table; their size can be changed, and they can be laid on top of each other, again as if they were papers spread on a table. Hence, a window handler provides a powerful tool to view and to operate on many documents concurrently, and thereby enlarges the power of a screen to a very significant extent. The improvement is even more dramatic, if the window handler permits the selection of different character sizes and styles, large characters being used in windows that are predominantly used, small ones in less important documents or when a large section of text need be seen at once.

A good example of a user of several windows is a program debugger. In the pictures shown subsequently, windows are used for viewing the program text, the values of variables, storage dumps, the chain of activated procedures, the list of loaded modules, and for the dialog between programmer and computer.

The following definition module shows that its facilities are subdivided into procedures for manipulating windows (opening, closing, changing size and position, overlaying), for writing text, for drawing on the level of raster elements or individual characters, and for miscellaneous other actions.

```
DEFINITION MODULE WindowHandler;  (*Ch. Jacobi*)

EXPORT QUALIFIED
  Bitmap, Font, BlockDescriptor, Mode,
  Window, WindowDescriptor,
  OpenWindow, CloseWindow, ChangeWindow,
  UseForDefault, DefaultWindow, FullScreen, LoadFont,
  WriteChar, FreeChars, FreeLines,
  GetPos, SetPos, ClearChars, ClearLines,
  Replicate, BlockTransfer, DisplayDot, DisplayChar,
  SelectWindow, PutOnTop, TopWindow;

CONST N = 24;

TYPE
  Bitmap;
  Font;
  BlockDescriptor  = RECORD x,y,w,h: CARDINAL END ;
  Mode         = (replace, paint, invert, erase);
  Window        = POINTER TO WindowDescriptor;
  WindowHint;

WindowDescriptor =
 RECORD
   wptr:    WindowHint;
   bm:      Bitmap;
   font:    Font;
   next:    Window;(*downwards; depending on visibility*)
```

```
        header:   ARRAY [0..N-1] OF CHAR;
        outerblk: BlockDescriptor;
        innerblk: BlockDescriptor;
      END;
```

(* window descriptors are neither to be copied nor changed;
   inner- and outerblk denote the coordinates, widths and heights
   of the outside and inside rectangles of the widow frame *)

```
PROCEDURE OpenWindow(VAR w: Window; x,y, width, height: CARDINAL;
        name: ARRAY OF CHAR; VAR done: BOOLEAN);

PROCEDURE CloseWindow(VAR w: Window);

PROCEDURE ChangeWindow(w: Window; x,y, width, height: CARDINAL;
        VAR done: BOOLEAN);

PROCEDURE Clear(w: Window);

PROCEDURE UseForDefault(w: Window);

PROCEDURE DefaultWindow(): Window;

PROCEDURE FullScreen(): Window;

PROCEDURE WriteChar(w: Window; ch: CHAR);

PROCEDURE FreeChars(w: Window): CARDINAL;
  (* returns the number of free characters in the current line *)

PROCEDURE FreeLines(w: Window): CARDINAL;
  (* returns the number of empty lines not counting the current line*)

PROCEDURE GetPos(w: Window; VAR line, pos: CARDINAL);

PROCEDURE SetPos(w: Window; line, pos: CARDINAL);

PROCEDURE ClearChars(w: Window; n: CARDINAL);
  (* clears n positions but at most the rest of the current line *)

PROCEDURE ClearLines(w: Window; n: CARDINAL);
  (* clears n full lines but at least the rest of the current line *)

PROCEDURE LoadFont(w: Window;
        fontName: ARRAY OF CHAR; VAR ok: BOOLEAN);

PROCEDURE Replicate(w: Window; VAR dest: BlockDescriptor;
         m: Mode; VAR pattern: ARRAY OF WORD);
  (* a pattern contains the size of its image in the first word,
     followed by the image of width 16*)
```

```
      PROCEDURE BlockTransfer(dw: Window; VAR dest: BlockDescriptor;
        m: Mode; sw: Window; VAR source: BlockDescriptor);

      PROCEDURE DisplayDot(w: Window; x, y: CARDINAL; m: Mode);

      PROCEDURE DisplayChar(w: Window; VAR lineBlk: BlockDescriptor;
            VAR f: Font; ch: CHAR);

      PROCEDURE SelectWindow(VAR w: Window;
        x,y: CARDINAL; VAR found: BOOLEAN);
      (* Returns the window in which the point x,y is visible*)

      PROCEDURE PutOnTop(w: Window);

      PROCEDURE TopWindow(): Window;
        (* to get a list of all windows start with TopWindow and
         follow the next fields of the WindowDescriptors; the list
         is ordered according to visibility *)
    END WindowHandler.
```

The procedure OpenWindow generates a new window with given position and size. The parameter name specifies a text string that appears in the window's heading. ChangeWindow allows to alter a window's position and size, and CloseWindow deletes the specified window.

When a window handler is used, it must continue to allow the use of the standard output procedures for writing text, for they are typically used by an underlying operating system, and possibly by other standard modules for transmitting messages to the user. Hence, one of the opened windows must be designated as the so-called default window in which text is written when no specific window is indicated. Such a designation is performed by calling UseForDefault.

For writing text sequentially in windows, the procedure WriteChar(w,ch) is provided. The writing position (relative to the window's origin) can be inspected by calling GetPos and determined by SetPos. The procedures FreeChars and FreeLines are used to determine the space left for further writing in the window, and ClearChars and ClearLines for erasing space following the current writing position. These procedures are intended for use only with a character style (font) with a fixed, identical width for all characters.

For operations other than sequential text output, four basic procedures are provided. Replicate causes a rectangular pattern to be copied and replicated over an area specified by a so-called *block descriptor* indicating the coordinates of the lower left corner, the width and height. BlockTransfer copies a rectangular area into another one. DisplayDot writes a single dot. DisplayChar writes a dot pattern taken from a so-called *font* depicting a given character.

In concluding, we shall try to formulate a few useful guidelines for the design of programs that carry a dialog with their user. This dialog is based on input from the keyboard and a pointing device (Mouse) and output to a screen, with or without windows.

1. Precede any text input request by the output of a string indicating the meaning of the answer.

2. Allow for corrections by typing the deletion character DEL, and request termination of

the input by specific characters such as RETURN or blank.

3. Reserve a specific character (usually ESC) for termination of the program.

4. If a pointing device is used, reserve the keyboard for text input (which usually serves as a parameter to commands), and accept commands primarily through the pointing device using the menu technique.

5. Keep menus short; do not exceed 8 commands. Remember that the shown menu may depend on the current position of the cursor, i.e. it may directly relate to the pointed object or environment.

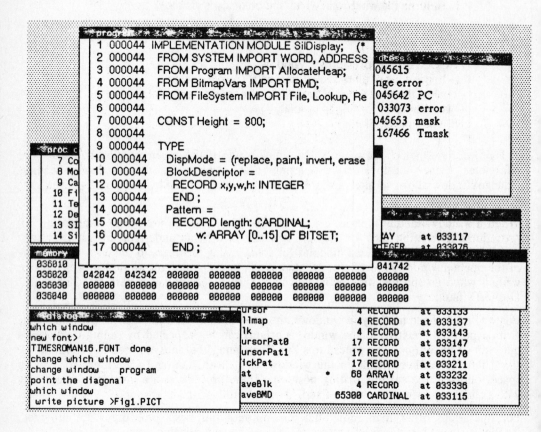

29. Low-level facilities

High-level languages encourage and even force the programmer to conceive his programs in a structured fashion. Structured statements provide a high degree of order and perspicuity of the programmed algorithmic text. Structured data declarations allow a high level of abstraction in the organization of a program's data and their organization in terms that are appropriate for the problem at hand. The principal advantage is additional safety against mistakes, because structure provides redundancy which can (and must) be used by implementations - in particular compilers - to detect inconsistencies of the program which become manifest as violations of language rules. In this respect, the concept of data types is particularly powerful and is therefore the primary characteristic of high-level programming languages.

However, we recognize the existence of applications where the rules of a language as presented in the preceding chapters are too restrictive. These are typically applications where data of some given structure are to be viewed as having some other structure, i.e. where their representation is not a priori determined by some declaration specified in the high-level language. Included are also those cases where the data structure has to satisfy conditions imposed by a particular computer system, in short, where machine-dependent specifications are to be considered. Data that have been generated by a program not written in Modula, or by a Modula program operating on a different computer, are typically known only as structures described in terms of computer-dependent entities.

Another case arises when programs are to be written for computers that reserve specific storage locations for particular purposes. If these locations are to be accessed, we need to be able to indicate their place in the store.

Since Modula-2 is intended as a general purpose language capable of expressing also problems of the kind just mentioned, it must provide adequate facilities. These are called *low-level facilities,* because they represent considerations at a low level of abstraction close to the computer being used. Their subsequent description must therefore inherently be incomplete. We can merely specify their general nature; the details have to be supplied by documents about specific, individual implementations.

The primary characteristic of low-level facilities is that they lack redundancy and are therefore **not** checked for consistency with language rules. A programmer using such facilites is therefore much less protected against errors. He is strongly advised to resort to these facilities only in cases where their use is clearly unavoidable, because the regular language facilities do not cater to the problem.

Foremost is the facility to breach Modula's type system: type identifiers can be used as function identifiers denoting a *type transfer function.* Such a function is considered as transferring a value of the type given by the parameter into the corresponding value of the type specified by the function identifier. For example, the value of an expression c of type CARDINAL is mapped into its corresponding value of type INTEGER by the function INTEGER(c). The function BITSET(c) yields the corresponding value of type BITSET. The correspondences are **not** defined by the language Modula. They must be supplied by additional, system-dependent information. The key idea behind these type tranfers is, however, that they do not involve any actual computation. Hence, in the above examples, INTEGER(c) is used, if the bit pattern representing the cardinal value c is to be interpreted as an integer, and BITSET(c) is used, if it is to be interpreted as a bitset. The programmer must therefore be aware of the computer-internal representations of the involved data types. The functions have the purpose of indicating the intended interpretation and of disabling the compiler's type checking and error reporting system.

Also among the low-level facilities are two basic data types to be discussed in more detail. They are called WORD and ADDRESS. Every computer's store is a sequence of so-called *words,* each word being an individually addressable unit consisting of a fixed number of bits. Data declared in Modula are mapped by the compiler onto one or several words. Modula does not allow any operators to be applied to data of type WORD (except assignment), because such a value is considered as not interpreted. However, the use of type transfer functions mentioned above makes operators applicable to words too, because the function identifier exhibits the intended interpretation. Obviously, such use of the type WORD is rendering the program highly dependent on implementations, because on some computers a word may consist of as few as 8 bits, whereas on others a word may consist of many more bits. The use of this type therefore automatically makes a program non-portable.

If a parameter of a procedure is given the type WORD, its corresponding actual parameter may be of any type that assigns a single word to its variables. No type transfer need be explicitly specified in the call. For example, the procedures ReadWord and WriteWord of the modules Streams and FileSystem previously introduced specify a parameter of type WORD. They allow the reading and writing of sequences of words and their interpretation according to the types of actual parameters supplied. These types may differ among various calls. Given this facility, it becomes possible to read files with data formatted according to rules not expressible in terms of Modula data structures. As a simple example, consider the task of reading a file, whose first word indicates the file length, and which is followed by word pairs whose first element is a number, the second a bitset. Assuming that both cardinal and bitset values occupy a single word, this task is formulated as follows:

```
ReadWord(in,length); length : = length -1;
WHILE length > 1 DO
  ReadWord(in,num); ReadWord(in,set);
  process(num, set); length : = length -2
END
```

The rule that a formal parameter of type WORD is compatible with any type of actual parameter (as long as that type occupies a single storage word) is extended in the case of an open array with element type WORD. Specifically, if a formal parameter is specified as ARRAY OF WORD, then any variable, structured or unstructured, can be supplied as actual parameter. The use of this facility requires exact knowledge of a compiler's mapping of data structures into sequences of words. The number of words used for a variable is SIZE(v), that of any variable of type T is TSIZE(T). Both SIZE and TSIZE are functions which must be imported from the standard module SYSTEM.

Note: On the PDP-11, TSIZE(WORD) = 2, since the addressable unit of store is the byte.

The type ADDRESS denotes values used as addresses for words, and it is defined as

TYPE ADDRESS = POINTER TO WORD

The word addressed by an address a can now be denoted by a↑, where ↑ is the dereferencing operator used with regular pointers. Values of type ADDRESS are considered as assignment compatible with all pointer types. This rule is particularly important in conjunction with parameters: if a formal parameter is of type ADDRESS, its corresponding actual parameter may be of any pointer type. An immediate consequence is again the removal of any type checking safety, when this type is introduced.

In addition, arithmetic operators can be applied to operands of type ADDRESS as if they were of type CARDINAL. This facility allows, among other things, the formulation of storage management programs. Assume, for instance, that a sequence of words is to be read from a file and loaded into the store at addresses org, org+1, ... Let the first word again specify the length of the sequence. The function ADR(x) delivers the address of the variable x, where x can be of any type.

```
ReadWord(in,length);
length : = length -1; a : = ADR(buffer);
WHILE length > 0 DO
  ReadWord(in,a↑); a : = a + 1; length : = length -1
END
```

The types WORD and ADDRESS must also be imported from module SYSTEM. This requirement ensures that programs making use of these low-level types be clearly marked in their heading. The module SYSTEM contains data types and associated procedures which are governed by exceptional rules that need be known by the compiler. Hence, SYSTEM is intimately connected with the compiler instead of being supplied as a separate module, and it is therefore called a pseudo module. It can, however, be considered as if it were defined by the following definition module:

```
DEFINITION MODULE SYSTEM;
  EXPORT QUALIFIED
    WORD, ADDRESS, PROCESS,
    ADR, SIZE, TSIZE,
    NEWPROCESS, TRANSFER, ... ;

  TYPE WORD; ADDRESS; PROCESS;
  PROCEDURE ADR(x: AnyType): ADDRESS;       (* the address of x *)
  PROCEDURE SIZE(VAR v: AnyType): CARDINAL; (* the number of words *)
  PROCEDURE TSIZE(AnyType): CARDINAL;       (* the number of words *)

  PROCEDURE NEWPROCESS(P: PROC; A: ADDRESS; n: CARDINAL; VAR q: PROCESS);
  PROCEDURE TRANSFER(VAR p,q: PROCESS);

  ...
END SYSTEM.
```

The dots imply that this module may contain further facilities depending on each individual implementation. The type PROCESS and the procedures NEWPROCESS and TRANSFER will be explained in the subsequent chapter.

Implementations of Modula may, but do not have to provide a facility to specify a fixed address for a variable. If this facility is provided, the address is specified immediately following the variable identifier in its declaration. Examples are contained in the following chapter.

30. Concurrent processes and coroutines

In this chapter we introduce concepts for multiprogramming, i.e. the programming of several, concurrently executed computations. These facilities are deliberately restricted to the formulation of so-called *loosely coupled* processes. We exclude the area of tightly coupled arrays of processes, considering their field of application as fairly narrow and specialized. Instead, we restrict the discussion to programs that describe several processes that interact relatively infrequently, and are therefore said to be loosely coupled. By infrequently is meant that interaction occurs at a few, well-defined, explicit points in the program, and by a process we understand a sequence of actions, i.e. an inherently sequential process. Programming as encountered so far can therefore be considered as a special case involving one single process only. Inversely, we can inherit for multiprogramming all facilities and techniques learned so far, and we need to add merely a few facilities for the designation of concurrent processes and for their interaction. In this regard we follow the tradition of earlier languages for multiprogramming such as *Modula-1* and Brinch Hansen's *Concurrent Pascal*.

Generally, one distinguishes between the following kinds of multiprogramming systems:

1. The computer consists of *several identical* processors. The programmed processes are executed in *genuine concurrency*.

2. The computer consists of a *single* processor only. It acts on a single process at any instance of time and is switched among processes, i.e. it is time-multiplexed. (A more general case is a system where m processors serve to execute n processes, where m is usually much less than n.) The processes are said to be *quasi-concurrent*.

3. *Several* processors of *different* capability serve to execute several processes. Some processes are such that some of their parts can be executed by specific processors only. Typical examples of such special purpose processors are input/output devices.

Our goal is to find a concept and a notation that lets us express the common aspects of all three kinds of systems in identical terms at a high level of abstraction. To a certain degree, we may regard the differences between kinds 1 and 2 as a matter of implementation only. More specifically, if we formulate the logical processes and their interaction in a way that they may be executed in genuine concurrency, then a system housing a single processor may just as well be used to execute the processes quasi-concurrently. Case 3, however, needs special treatment, because evidently the existence of processors with distinct capabilities cannot be hidden as a mere detail of implementation.

In this chapter, we discuss the formulation of processes and their interaction in terms of Modula-2. Furthermore, we present an implementation based on single-processor computers and the concept of the coroutine, i.e. a system offering quasi-concurrency. The programming of special purpose devices (for input and output) and their operating in genuine concurrency is deferred to the subsequent chapter.

For the use of concurrent processes we introduce the module *Processes*. It has the advantage that it offers the necessary facilities for multiprogramming at a high level of abstraction virtually without necessitating any additional language constructs. It provides the facilities of Modula-1 and most of Concurrent Pascal's.

```
        DEFINITION MODULE Processes;
         EXPORT QUALIFIED SIGNAL,
          StartProcess, SEND, WAIT, Awaited, Init;

        TYPE SIGNAL;

        PROCEDURE StartProcess(P: PROC; n: CARDINAL);
         (*start a concurrent process with program P and workspace of size n.
          PROC is a standard type defined as  PROC = PROCEDURE *)

        PROCEDURE SEND(VAR s: SIGNAL);
         (*one process waiting for s is resumed*)

        PROCEDURE WAIT(VAR s: SIGNAL);
         (*wait for some other process to send s*)

        PROCEDURE Awaited(s: SIGNAL): BOOLEAN;
         (*Awaited(s) = "at least one process is waiting for s" *)

        PROCEDURE Init(VAR s: SIGNAL);
         (*compulsory initialization*)
        END Processes.
```

A call StartProcess(P,n) starts the execution of a process which is expressed by a procedure P. Whether this process is executed in genuine or quasi-concurrency of course depends on the implementation of Processes used. Every process requires a certain workspace in the store to allocate its local variables. The size of the workspace in terms of the number of words is n; it is to be chosen depending on the number of local variables and local calls used in this process. (A typical minimal workspace size is 100 words.)

Communication among processes occurs in two distinct ways, namely via common, *shared variables,* and via so-called *signals.* Common variables are used to transfer data among processes, and raise the problem of harmonious cooperation. No process should meddle with common variables while another is performing some critical action upon them. A reasonable solution to this problem is to encapsulate common variables in a module which guarantees mutual exclusion of processes. Such a module is called a *monitor* and will be discussed below. Signals, exported as a data type from the module Processes, carry themselves no data, but serve to synchronize processes. Only two operations are applicable to signals (apart from the compulsory initialization): a process may send a signal and it may wait for (some other process sending) a signal. Every signal denotes a certain condition or state among the program's variables, and sending the signal must imply that this condition has arisen. We highly recommend that its associated condition be specified as a comment with the signal's declaration. A process waiting for a signal may then assume that this condition has been met whenever the process is resumed. The sending of a signal reactivates at most one process. (Otherwise one of the awakened processes might quickly invalidate the condition, causing the other processes to proceed on false premises). Sending a signal for which no process is waiting is considered as a null operation.

The programmer should be aware, without caring about the details of their implementation, that on systems using quasi-concurrency, calls of SEND and WAIT (may) imply a switch of the processor from the calling process to another (waiting) process, and that these are the only occasions where such switches occur. Waiting for certain conditions to arise must therefore never be programmed in terms of empty loops, so-called *busy waiting,* but rather using explicit calls of WAIT.

Another important programming rule is that shared variables be declared and hidden within monitors. A monitor is a module which guarantees mutual exclusion of processes and thereby can ensure integrity of its local data. Access to these data is - because they are hidden - restricted to statements of the monitor's (exported) procedures, and since the monitor guarantees that a calling process is temporarily delayed while another process is executing any one of the monitor's procedures, mutual exclusion of data access is automatically achieved. A module is designated to be a monitor by specifying a *priority* in its heading. The priority value is a cardinal number; here it suffices to know that any number causes the module to become a monitor.

The following example is supposed to illustrate the rules given so far. It embodies a classical problem of multiprogramming, namely that of exchanging data among various processes. This typically involves the use of a *buffer* ; the larger the buffer is, the more loosely are the processes coupled. We assume that processes may deposit data elements in the buffer and fetch elements from the buffer. The buffer is the principal shared variable; together with the operations deposit and fetch it is encapsulated in a monitor. Since we do not know - neither do we have to nor do we wish to - the particularities of the involved processes, we can immediately focus our attention on the core of the multiprogramming problem, namely this monitor which handles the process cooperation. The processes themselves contain calls of fetch and deposit and are typically cyclic. These calls embody their interaction. If a process contains calls of deposit, it is a *producer.* Processes with calls of fetch are said to be *consumers.*

The buffer is here declared as an array variable used in a circular manner. Two conditions for waiting arise: a producer calling deposit may find the buffer full, or a consumer calling fetch may find it empty. These two conditions give rise to the declaration of the two signals called *nonempty* and *nonfull* used to reactivate a waiting process. The monitor Buffer is here programmed as a local module, and n is the number of data items deposited in the buffer.

```
MODULE Buffer [1];
  EXPORT deposit, fetch;
  IMPORT SIGNAL, SEND, WAIT, Init, ElementType;

  CONST N = 128; (*buffer size*)
  VAR n: [0..N]; (*no. of deposited elements*)
    nonfull: SIGNAL;  (* n < N *)
    nonempty: SIGNAL; (* n > 0 *)
    in, out: [0..N-1]; (*indices*)
    buf: ARRAY [0..N-1] OF ElementType;

  PROCEDURE deposit(x: ElementType);
  BEGIN
    IF n = N THEN WAIT(nonfull) END;
    (* n < N *) n := n + 1; (* 0 < n <= N *)
    buf[in] : = x; in : = (in + 1) MOD N;
    SEND(nonempty)
```

```
  END deposit;

  PROCEDURE fetch(VAR x: ElementType);
  BEGIN
    IF n = 0 THEN WAIT(nonempty) END;
    (* n > 0 *) n := n-1; (* 0 <= n < N *)
    x := buf[out]; out := (out + 1) MOD N;
    SEND(nonfull)
  END fetch;

BEGIN n := 0; in := 0; out := 0;
  Init(nonfull); Init(nonempty)
END Buffer
```

The presented version of the buffering algorithm has the unappealing property of sending a signal each time when an element is deposited or fetched. However, in principle a synchronization signal need only be sent, if a partner is waiting. It is a good principle to minimize the number of signal exchanges and thereby to reduce the degree of coupling of processes. An improvement in this direction is achieved by Dijkstra's "sleeping barber" version. It extends the value range of the variable n with the following meanings, valid whenever no process has entered the monitor:

$n < 0$:   buffer is empty and -n consumers are waiting
$0 <= n <= N$:   n buffer slots are filled, no process is waiting
$N < n$:   buffer is full and n-N producers are waiting

The two procedures are now declared as

```
  PROCEDURE deposit(x: ElementType);
  BEGIN n := n + 1;
    IF n > N THEN WAIT(nonfull) END;
    (* n <= N *)
    buf[in] := x; in := (in + 1) MOD N;
    IF n <= 0 THEN SEND(nonempty) END
  END deposit;

  PROCEDURE fetch(VAR x: ElementType);
  BEGIN n := n-1;
    IF n < 0 THEN WAIT(nonempty) END;
    (* n >= 0 *)
    x := buf[out]; out := (out + 1) MOD N;
    IF n >= N THEN SEND(nonfull) END
  END fetch
```

We now turn our attention to the problem of implementation of the module Processes and present a possible solution. We emphasize that this is only one among many possibilities. It is designed for a single-processor computer, and this processor is time-shared to serve the processes. The solution is based on the concept of the *coroutine*. A coroutine is a sequential program essentially like a process as discussed above. The conceptual differences between the process and the coroutine can be summarized as follows.

1. Coroutines are known to be executed quasi-concurrently. Therefore their use avoids

the difficult problem of interaction of genuinely concurrent processes.

2. The processor is switched from one coroutine to another coroutine by an explicit *transfer statement.* Execution of the destination coroutine resumes at the point where it was suspended by its own last transfer statement.

It is evident that on a single-processor computer a process can be implemented as a coroutine, which emerges as a lower level concept. Its proximity to actual computers is evidenced by the transfer statement corresponding to a jump of control. Such a coroutine jump must store the current state of the current coroutine, which is said to be *suspended,* such that it can be properly *resumed* when another coroutine transfers control back to the suspended one. In every transfer, the destination coroutine is explicitly identified, and this contrasts with the WAIT and SEND statements used for synchronizing processes.

Because in Modula coroutines are considered as low-level facilities, their associated type and its operators have to be imported from the module SYSTEM (see chapter on low-level facilities). There are in particular the type PROCESS and the procedure TRANSFER. (Apologies to the reader for the unfortunate choice of the name PROCESS denoting coroutines.)

The heading of the transfer procedure is declared as

PROCEDURE TRANSFER(VAR source, destination: PROCESS);

Its call causes the source to be suspended - in order to be resumed later on with the statement following the transfer - and the destination to be resumed at its current point of suspension. In order to create a coroutine, the procedure NEWPROCESS is to be called.

PROCEDURE NEWPROCESS(P: PROC; A: ADDRESS; n: CARDINAL; VAR new: PROCESS)

Here P denotes the parameterless procedure which constitutes the program for the newly created coroutine. A is the origin address of a workspace needed to allocate the local variables of the coroutine and to store the coroutine's state while it is suspended; n denotes the size of this workspace in storage units. The call assigns to the variable new (a reference to) the created coroutine whose state is initialized such that, when control is transferred to it, execution starts at the beginning of P. Hence, coroutines are started by an explicit transfer; they must also be terminated by such a transfer.

We are now in a position to present an implementation of the module Processes in terms of coroutines. The essential aspect is that calls of WAIT and SEND have to be translated into transfers, in which the destination must be identified. Consequently, the module Processes must embody a process administration that distributes the processor's time in a fair strategy among the processes. This administration is called a *scheduler.* Normally, it is part of a computer's operating system. Indeed, individual implementations of Modula have the freedom to prohibit the introduction of coroutines and to restrict the programmer to the use of the high-level concepts presented by the module Processes.

```
IMPLEMENTATION MODULE Processes [1];
  FROM SYSTEM IMPORT ADDRESS, TSIZE, PROCESS, NEWPROCESS, TRANSFER;
  FROM Storage IMPORT ALLOCATE;

  TYPE SIGNAL = POINTER TO ProcessDescriptor;

  ProcessDescriptor =
  RECORD next: SIGNAL; (*ring*)
```

```
  queue: SIGNAL; (*queue of waiting processes*)
  cor:  PROCESS;
  ready: BOOLEAN
 END ;

VAR cp: SIGNAL; (*current process*)

PROCEDURE StartProcess(P: PROC; n: CARDINAL);
 VAR s0: SIGNAL; wsp: ADDRESS;
BEGIN s0 : = cp; ALLOCATE(wsp, n);
 ALLOCATE(cp, TSIZE(ProcessDescriptor));
 WITH cp↑ DO
  next : = s0↑.next; s0↑.next : = cp;
  ready : = TRUE; queue : = NIL
 END ;
 NEWPROCESS(P, wsp, n, cp↑.cor); TRANSFER(s0↑.cor, cp↑.cor)
END StartProcess;

PROCEDURE SEND(VAR s: SIGNAL);
 VAR s0: SIGNAL;
BEGIN
 IF s # NIL THEN
  s0 : = cp; cp : = s;
  WITH cp↑ DO
   s : = queue; ready : = TRUE; queue : = NIL
  END ;
  TRANSFER(s0↑.cor, cp↑.cor)
 END
END SEND;

PROCEDURE WAIT(VAR s: SIGNAL);
 VAR s0, s1: SIGNAL;
BEGIN (*insert cp in queue s*)
 IF s = NIL THEN s : = cp
 ELSE s0 : = s; s1 : = s0↑.queue;
  WHILE s1 # NIL DO
   s0 : = s1; s1 : = s0↑.queue
  END ;
  s0↑.queue : = cp
 END ;
 s0 : = cp;
 REPEAT cp : = cp↑.next UNTIL cp↑.ready;
 IF cp = s0 THEN (*deadlock*) HALT END ;
 s0↑.ready : = FALSE; TRANSFER(s0↑.cor, cp↑.cor)
END WAIT;

PROCEDURE Awaited(s: SIGNAL): BOOLEAN;
BEGIN RETURN s # NIL
END Awaited;

PROCEDURE Init(VAR s: SIGNAL);
```

```
    BEGIN s : = NIL
    END Init;

  BEGIN ALLOCATE(cp, TSIZE(ProcessDescriptor));
    WITH cp↑ DO
      next : = cp; ready : = TRUE; queue : = NIL
    END
  END Processes.
```

When a process is started with a call of StartProcess(P,n), a descriptor of the process and a workspace for its associated coroutine are allocated. The descriptor is inserted in a circular list (ring) containing all process descriptors created so far. The variable cp designates (the descriptor of) the currently executed process. By traversing the ring, any process can be reached. The successor process is denoted by the descriptor's field called *next.*

The crucial question is that of the representation of signals. Whereas at the user's level of abstraction a signal represents an arising condition, it represents at the level of implementation the set of processes that are waiting for the signal. Since the number of these processes is unknown, a sensible solution is to organize them as a linked list. Hence, a signal variable represents the head of the list, and every process descriptor contains a field linking to the next process waiting for that same signal. Its value is of course NIL, if no such process exists.

From this description, the functions of the procedures SEND and WAIT become obvious. SEND(s) takes the first element off the list s and transfers control from the sending process (identified by cp) to that process. WAIT(s) appends the calling process (again identified by cp) at the end of the list s. Appending at the end embodies the requested fairness, ensuring that waiting processes cannot overtake other processes waiting for the same signal, because the list represents a first-in first-out queue. In principle, any process which is not waiting could now be resumed. Fairness is here achieved by simply proceeding through the ring starting at cp; the additional descriptor field called ready is used to quickly determine whether or not a process is ready for resumption. (This solution is preferred to the removal of waiting processes from the ring requiring their reinsertion when they are reactivated. This preference is based on the assumption that the number of processes is reasonably small.)

In principle, process interaction should be confined to a monitor, i.e. a module guaranteeing mutual exclusion. However, because we have stipulated that this module be implemented on a single-processor computer, concurrent interaction is by definition impossible, and therefore the specification of a monitor, i.e. of a priority in the module's heading, is redundant.

31. Device handling, concurrency, and interrupts

In the last chapter we have discussed systems with several processes and how to simulate concurrent processes by time-sharing a single processor. Now we consider the inverse situation, where several processors participate in the execution of a single process. For the sake of simplicity, let us look at a cyclic process consisting of a producing and a consuming part. Let the process be formulated as

> LOOP produce(x); consume(x) END

Now assume that each part can be executed by a specific processor only. We recognize that at any time only one of the two processors can be active. Hence they need to be synchronized, which is easily accomplished by the introduction of a synchronization variable s with the meaning of, say, "the consumer is active" (and with initial value FALSE). Each of the two sequential processors is now describable by its own program, which is again cyclic.

> Producer:
>   LOOP wait(NOT s);
>   produce(x); s : = TRUE
>   END
>
> Consumer:
>   LOOP wait(s);
>   consume(x); s : = FALSE
>   END

The operation wait(b) can be understood as equivalent to the statement

> REPEAT (*polling*) UNTIL b

and the variables x and s constitute the interface. These variables are usually implemented as special hardware registers, called *device registers*. In some computers, they are accessed by special commands - to be made available in their Modula implementations by special procedures. In other computers, they appear as if they were locations of the memory and are given fixed addressed (so-called *memory-mapped I/O*).

As example, we shall now consider the interaction of a keyboard input process with a "regular" consumer process programmed for the PDP-11 computer. The PDP-11 uses memory-mapped IO registers. Its keyboard status variable s, for instance, is represented by bit 7 of the word with address 777560B, the buffer variable x by bits 0 - 7 of the word with address 777562B. Because the PDP-11 computer has (potentially) many such interface registers, its Modula implementation offers the possibility to specify a variable's address in its declaration, as the following examples show. We *strongly urge* programmers to restrict the use of this facility to variables representing such device registers, and to refrain from its misuse for other purposes. The two pertinent registers are introduced by the following declarations:

> VAR s [777560B]: BITSET;

```
        x [777562B]: CHAR
```

Whereas the producer's program is implemented by hardware, the consumer's is formulated by the schema

```
        LOOP
          REPEAT UNTIL 7 IN s;
          consume(x)
        END
```

The lack of the statement "s := TRUE" is explained by the circumstance that the PDP-11's keyboard interface is designed such that access to x automatically also sets s.

This concludes the presentation of the simple example of keyboard handling by polling.

The drawback of the scheme presented is that the two processors are very tightly coupled; they strictly alternate. While one of them is active, the other sleeps. In general, better decoupling is desirable. It is achieved by providing a buffer, preferrably one with a reasonably large number of slots. For operating the buffer, we employ the producer/consumer scheme explained in the preceding chapter. Both partners are represented as coroutines.

The principal question now arising is the following. When do coroutine transfers occur, - i.e. when are signals exchanged - in order to keep both processors - the computer and the device - as active as possible and as loosely coupled as possible?

To make the problem and its solution more explicit, we return to the concrete example involving the keyboard as producer. The consumer alternates between the operations of fetching and consuming an element. Both statements are executed by the general-purpose, programmed processor. The producer alternates between producing and depositing an element. The latter operation is also performed by the main processor; production, however, is done by the keyboard. We assume - and this is characteristic for loosely coupled processes - that depositing and fetching takes a negligible amount of time compared to producing and consuming. Therefore, we may consider the producer process as being executed by the keyboard processor, only occasionally requiring the service of the main processor, which can be borrowed from its principal task unhesitatingly because of the negligible amount of time it will be engaged. The answer to the previously posed question now emerges:

The programmable processor is transferred from the consumer (main) process whenever the keyboard has performed its part of the producer process, and it is transferred back as soon as the deposit action is terminated.

The return transfer can be programmed explicitly as a TRANSFER statement. This, however, is **not** the case for the transfer from the consumer to the producer, because the current point of control is unknown a priori. In fact, we must be able to interrupt the execution of the consumer wherever control currently lies. In terms of Modula: we must be able to insert a transfer statement at an arbitrary, not previously specifyable point.

Most computers offer exactly this possibility; the unprogrammed transfer is called an *interrupt*. To illustrate its use, we formulate the two processes used as example so far. We shall regard the consumer as the main program, and are only interested in its fetch part which picks the next element from the buffer and which is therefore formulated as a procedure. The producer appears as a coroutine communicating with the keyboard through its interface variable x. Together with the deposit part of the producer it represents the interface between the two partners and is therefore encapsulated within a monitor module hiding the buffer (see preceding chapter). Whereas the fetch action is expressed as a procedure, the deposit action is programmed in-line with the producer coroutine, which is held within the monitor in its entirety, because the produce action, executed by the keyboard, is considered as exempt from the rule of mutual exclusion. This coroutine represents what is often called an *interrupt handler*.

```
MODULE Keyboard [4];
  EXPORT fetch, n (*read only*);
  IMPORT ADR, SIZE, WORD, PROCESS,
    NEWPROCESS, TRANSFER, IOTRANSFER;

  CONST N = 32;

  VAR x [777562B]: CHAR;   (*keyboard data*)
    s [777560B]: BITSET;  (*keyboard status*)

  VAR n, in, out: CARDINAL;
    buf: ARRAY [0..N-1] OF CHAR;
    PRO, CON: PROCESS;
    wsp: ARRAY [0..177B] OF WORD;

  PROCEDURE fetch(VAR ch: CHAR);
  BEGIN (*to be called only, if n > 0*)
    IF n > 0 THEN
      ch : = buf[out]; out : = (out + 1) MOD N;
      n : = n-1
    ELSE ch : = 0C
    END
  END fetch;

  PROCEDURE producer; (*acts as coroutine*)
  BEGIN
    LOOP IOTRANSFER(PRO, CON, 60B)
      (*character being typed on keyboard; reception of character causes
        insertion of TRANSFER(CON,PRO) in consumer program ( = interrupt)
        and the producer's resumption at this point*)
      IF n < N THEN
        buf[in] : = x; in : = (in + 1) MOD N;
        n : = n + 1
        (*ignore characters when buffer is full*)
      END
    END
  END producer;

  BEGIN n : = 0; in : = 0; out : = 0;
    NEWPROCESS(producer, ADR(wsp), SIZE(wsp), PRO);
    EXCL(s,6); TRANSFER(CON,PRO)
  END Keyboard
```

The above module is formulated for the PDP-11 computer, as it references implementation

138

dependent facilities, in particular the keyboard interface variables x and s. Three details need mentioning:

1. The transfer returning control from the interrupting coroutine (producer) to the interrupted coroutine (consumer) must be expressed by the statement

IOTRANSFER(source, destination, va)

where va is an additional parameter denoting the interrupting device's so-called *interrupt vector* address as prescribed by the hardware.

2. Each device's interrupting capability must explicitly be enabled. This is done by the statement EXCL(s,6), which resets the interrupt disabling bit in the keyboard status register. From this point on, an interrupt, i.e. an immediate transfer of control to the producer coroutine occurs, whenever a key is depressed.

3. It is of course essential to prohibit unscheduled transfers at points where they could be harmful. They must be banned from critical operations performed on shared variables. Hence, all such operations are placed inside a monitor, and the monitor must guarantee non-interruptability of its parts. This level is expressed by specifying an *interrupt priority* as dictated by the served device, which is 4 in the case of the keyboard on the PDP-11. (Note that shutting out interrupts is a simple technique for achieving mutual exclusion.)

4. Computers featuring a so-called *priority interrupt system* allow to turn off interrupt signals selectively according to assigned priorities. Specifically, each interrupt source is given an individual but fixed priority q. The processor, instead of having an on/off state only, has a level of interruptibility p, implying that the processor can be interrupted by signals with priority $q > p$ only.

And this concludes the exposition of the use of coroutines and interrupt-driven transfers of control with the example of a keyboard input. In concluding, we add that what was here expressed as a cyclic process is often called an interrupt handler, whose cyclic nature is hidden by the coroutine transfer's inclusion of a return jump. We much favour the explicit notation of the cyclic process, and in particular emphasize that it is most appropriate to consider interrupts as unscheduled coroutine transfers.

Also, we need to mention that on many computer systems the operating of peripheral devices - and therefore the use of interrupts - is the private domain of a resident operating system. On such computers, the programmer must not access these facilities, even if trespasses may go unreported, because this might seriously endanger the proper functionning of the operating system and thereby also of its clients. However, Modula was conceived with the goal of serving in the construction of such operating systems as well. The inclusion of adequate device and interrupt handling facilities was therefore indispensible. Their use should nevertheless be confined to so-called stand-alone systems which do not have the support (nor the burden) of a given operating system.

Report on
The Programming Language Modula-2

1. Introduction

Modula-2 grew out of a practical need for a general, efficiently implementable systems programming language for minicomputers. Its ancestors are *Pascal* and *Modula*. From the latter it has inherited the name, the important module concept, and a systematic, modern syntax, from Pascal most of the rest. This includes in particular the data structures, i.e. arrays, records, variant records, sets, and pointers. Structured statements include the familiar if, case, repeat, while, for, and with statements. Their syntax is such that every structure ends with an explicit termination symbol.

The language is essentially machine-independent, with the exception of limitations due to wordsize. This appears to be in contradiction to the notion of a system-programming language, in which it must be possible to express all operations inherent in the underlying computer. The dilemma is resolved with the aid of the *module* concept. Machine-dependent items can be introduced in specific modules, and their use can thereby effectively be confined and isolated. In particular, the language provides the possibility to relax rules about data type compatibility in these cases. In a capable system-programming language it is possible to express input/output conversion procedures, file handling routines, storage allocators, process schedulers etc. Such facilities must therefore not be included as elements of the language itself, but appear as (so-called low-level) modules which are components of most programs written. Such a collection of standard modules is therefore an essential part of a Modula-2 implementation.

The concept of processes and their synchronization with signals as included in Modula is replaced by the lower-level notion of *coroutines* in Modula-2. It is, however, possible to formulate a (standard) module that implements such processes and signals. The advantage of not including them in the language itself is that the programmer may select a process scheduling algorithm tailored to his particular needs by programming that module on his own. Such a scheduler can even be entirely omitted in simple (but frequent) cases, e.g. when concurrent processes occur as device drivers only.

A modern system programming language should in particular also facilitate the construction of large programs, possibly designed by several people. The modules written by individuals should have well-specified interfaces that can be declared independently of their actual implementations. Modula-2 supports this idea by providing separate *definition* and *implementation modules*. The former define all objects exported from the corresponding implementation module; in some cases, such as procedures and types, the definition module specifies only those parts that are relevant to the interface, i.e. to the user or client of the module.

This report is not intended as a programmer's tutorial. It is intentionally kept concise, and (we hope) clear. Its function is to serve as a reference for programmers, implementors, and manual writers, and as an arbiter, should they find disagreement.

2. Syntax

A language is an infinite set of sentences, namely the sentences well formed according to its syntax. In Modula-2, these sentences are called *compilation units*. Each unit is a finite sequence of symbols from a finite *vocabulary*. The vocabulary of Modula-2 consists of identifiers, numbers, strings, operators, and delimiters. They are called lexical *symbols* and are composed of sequences of characters. (Note the distinction between symbols and characters.)

To describe the syntax, an extended Backus-Naur Formalism called EBNF is used. Angular brackets [ ] denote optionality of the enclosed sentential form, and curly brackets { } denote its repetition (possibly 0 times). Syntactic entities (non-terminal symbols) are denoted by English words expressing their intuitive meaning. Symbols of the language vocabulary (terminal symbols) are strings enclosed in quote marks or words written in capital letters, so-called *reserved words*. Syntactic rules (productions) are designated by a $ sign at the left margin of the line.

3. Vocabulary and representation

The representation of symbols in terms of characters depends on the underlying character set. The ASCII set is used in this paper, and the following lexical rules must be observed. Blanks must not occur within symbols (except in strings). Blanks and line breaks are ignored unless they are essential to separate two consecutive symbols.

1. *Identifiers* are sequences of letters and digits. The first character must be a letter.

$ ident = letter {letter | digit}.

Examples:

    x scan Modula ETH GetSymbol firstLetter

2. *Numbers* are (unsigned) integers or real numbers. Integers are sequences of digits. If the number is followed by the letter B, it is taken as an octal number; if it is followed by the letter H, it is taken as a hexadecimal number; if it is followed by the letter C, it denotes the character with the given (octal) ordinal number (and is of type CHAR, see 6.1).

An integer i in the range $0 <= i <=$ MaxInt can be considered as either of type INTEGER or CARDINAL; if it is in the range MaxInt $< i <=$ MaxCard, it is of type CARDINAL. For 16-bit computers: MaxInt = 32767, MaxCard = 65535.

A real number always contains a decimal point. Optionally it may also contain a decimal scale factor. The letter E is pronounced as "ten to the power of". A real number is of type REAL.

$ number = integer | real.
$ integer = digit {digit} | octalDigit {octalDigit} ("B"|"C")|
$ digit {hexDigit} "H".
$ real = digit {digit} "." {digit} [ScaleFactor].
$ ScaleFactor = "E" [" + "|"-"] digit {digit}.
$ hexDigit = digit |"A"|"B"|"C"|"D"|"E"|"F".
$ digit = octalDigit | "8"|"9".
$ octalDigit = "0"|"1"|"2"|"3"|"4"|"5"|"6"|"7".

Examples:

    1980 3764B 7BCH 33C 12.3 45.67E-8

3. *Strings* are sequences of characters enclosed in quote marks. Both double quotes and single quotes (apostrophes) may be used as quote marks. However, the opening and closing marks must be the same character, and this character cannot occur within the string. A string must not extend over the end of a line.

$ string = "'" {character} "'" | '"' {character} '"' .

A single-character string is of type CHAR, a string consisting of n>1 characters is of type

(see 6.4)

```
ARRAY [0..n-1] OF CHAR
```

Examples:

```
"MODULA"   "Don't worry!"   'codeword "Barbarossa"'
```

4. *Operators and delimiters* are the special characters, character pairs, or reserved words listed below. These reserved words consist exclusively of capital letters and MUST NOT be used in the role of identifiers. The symbols # and <> are synonyms, and so are & and AND.

+	=	AND	FOR	QUALIFIED
-	#	ARRAY	FROM	RECORD
*	<	BEGIN	IF	REPEAT
/	>	BY	IMPLEMENTATION	RETURN
:=	<>	CASE	IMPORT	SET
&	<=	CONST	IN	THEN
.	>=	DEFINITION	LOOP	TO
,	..	DIV	MOD	TYPE
;	:	DO	MODULE	UNTIL
(	)	ELSE	NOT	VAR
[	]	ELSIF	OF	WHILE
{	}	END	OR	WITH
↑	|	EXIT	POINTER	
		EXPORT	PROCEDURE	

5. *Comments* may be inserted between any two symbols in a program. They are arbitrary character sequences opened by the bracket (* and closed by *). Comments may be nested, and they do not affect the meaning of a program.

4. Declarations and scope rules

Every identifier occurring in a program must be introduced by a declaration, unless it is a standard identifier. The latter are considered to be predeclared, and they are valid in all parts of a program. For this reason they are called *pervasive*. Declarations also serve to specify certain permanent properties of an object, such as whether it is a constant, a type, a variable, a procedure, or a module.

The identifier is then used to refer to the associated object. This is possible in those parts of a program only which are within the so-called *scope* of the declaration. In general, the scope extends over the entire block (procedure or module declaration) to which the declaration belongs and to which the object is local. The scope rule is augmented by the following cases:

1. If an identifier x defined by a declaration D1 is used in another declaration (not statement) D2, then D1 must textually precede D2.

2. A type T1 can be used in a declaration of a pointer type T (see 6.7) which textually precedes the declaration of T1, if both T and T1 are declared in the same block. This is a relaxation of rule 1.

3. If an identifier defined in a module M1 is exported, the scope expands over the block which contains M1. If M1 is a compilation unit (see Ch. 14), it extends to all those units which import M1.

4. Field identifiers of a record declaration (see 6.5) are valid only in field designators and in with statements referring to a variable of that record type.

An identifier may be *qualified*. In this case it is prefixed by another identifier which designates the module (see Ch. 11) in which the qualified identifier is defined. The prefix and the identifier are separated by a period.

$ qualident = ident {"." ident}.

The following are standard identifiers:

ABS	(10.2)	HIGH	(10.2)
BITSET	(6.6)	INC	(10.2)
BOOLEAN	(6.1)	INCL	(10.2)
CAP	(10.2)	INTEGER	(6.1)
CARDINAL	(6.1)	NEW	(10.2)
CHAR	(6.1)	NIL	(6.7)
CHR	(10.2)	ODD	(10.2)
DEC	(10.2)	ORD	(10.2)
DISPOSE	(10.2)	PROC	(6.8)
EXCL	(10.2)	REAL	(6.1)
FALSE	(6.1)	TRUE	(6.1)
FLOAT	(10.2)	TRUNC	(10.2)
HALT	(10.2)	VAL	(10.2)

5. Constant declarations

A constant declaration associates an identifier with a constant value.

```
$  ConstantDeclaration = ident " = " ConstExpression.
$  ConstExpression = SimpleConstExpr [relation SimpleConstExpr].
$  relation = " = " | " # " | "<>" | "<" | "< = " | ">" | "> = " | IN .
$  SimpleConstExpr = [" + "|"-"] ConstTerm {AddOperator ConstTerm}.
$  AddOperator = " + " | "-" | OR .
$  ConstTerm = ConstFactor {MulOperator ConstFactor}.
$  MulOperator = "*" | "/" | DIV | MOD | AND | "&" .
$  ConstFactor = qualident | number | string | set |
$     "(" ConstExpression ")" | NOT ConstFactor.
$  set = [qualident] "{" [element {"," element}] "}".
$  element = ConstExpression [".." ConstExpression].
```

The meaning of operators is explained in Chapter 8. The identifier preceding the left brace of a set specifies the type of the set. If it is omitted, the standard type BITSET is assumed (see 6.6).

Examples of constant declarations are

```
N    = 100
limit = 2*N -1
all  = {0 .. WordSize-1}
```

6. Type declarations

A data type determines a set of values which variables of that type may assume, and it associates an identifier with the type. In the case of structured types, it also defines the structure of variables of this type. There are three different structures, namely arrays, records, and sets.

```
$  TypeDeclaration = ident " = " type.
$  type = SimpleType | ArrayType | RecordType | SetType |
$     PointerType | ProcedureType.
$  SimpleType = qualident | enumeration | SubrangeType.
```

Examples:

Color =	(red, green, blue)
Index =	[1 .. 80]
Card =	ARRAY Index OF CHAR
Node =	RECORD key: CARDINAL;
	left, right: TreePtr
	END
Tint =	SET OF Color
TreePtr =	POINTER TO Node
Function =	PROCEDURE(CARDINAL): CARDINAL

6.1. Basic types

The following basic types are predeclared and denoted by standard identifiers:

1. A variable of type INTEGER assumes as values the integers between *MinInt* and *MaxInt*.

2. A variable of type CARDINAL assumes as values the integers between 0 and *MaxCard*.

3. A variable of type BOOLEAN assumes the truth values TRUE or FALSE. These are the only values of this type.

4. A variable of type CHAR assumes as elements values of the character set provided by the used computer system.

5. A variable of type REAL assumes as values real numbers.

For implementations on 16-bit computers, MinInt = -32768, MaxInt = 32767, and MaxCard = 65535.

6.2. Enumerations

An enumeration is a list of identifiers that denote the values which constitute a data type. These identifiers are used as constants in the program. They, and no other values, belong to this type. The values are ordered, and the ordering relation is defined by their sequence in the enumeration. The ordinal number of the first value is 0.

```
$  enumeration = "(" IdentList ")".
$  IdentList = ident {"," ident}.
```

Examples of enumerations:

```
          (red, green, blue)
          (club, diamond, heart, spade)
          (Monday, Tuesday, Wednesday, Thursday, Friday, Saturday, Sunday)
```

6.3. Subrange types

A type T may be defined as a subrange of another, basic or enumeration type T1 (except REAL) by specification of the least and the highest value in the subrange.

```
$  SubrangeType = "[" ConstExpression ".." ConstExpression "]".
```

The first constant specifies the lower bound, and must not be greater than the upper bound. The type T1 of the bounds is called the *base type* of T, and all operators applicable to operands of type T1 are also applicable to operands of type T. However, a value to be assigned to a variable of a subrange type must lie within the specified interval. If the lower bound is a non-negative integer, the base type of the subrange is taken to be CARDINAL; if it is a negative integer, it is INTEGER.

A type T1 is said to be *compatible* with a type T0, if it is declared either as T1 = T0 or as a subrange of T0, or if T0 is a subrange of T1, or if T0 and T1 are both subranges of the same (base) type.

Examples of subrange types:

```
[0 .. N-1]
["A" .. "Z"]
[Monday .. Friday]
```

6.4. Array types

An array is a structure consisting of a fixed number of components which are all of the same type, called the *component type*. The elements of the array are designated by indices, values belonging to the *index type*. The array type declaration specifies the component type as well as the index type. The latter must be an enumeration, a subrange type, or one of the basic types BOOLEAN or CHAR.

$ ArrayType = ARRAY SimpleType {"," SimpleType} OF type.

A declaration of the form

```
ARRAY T1, T2, ... , Tn OF T
```

with n index types T1 ... Tn must be understood as an abbreviation for the declaration

```
ARRAY T1 OF
  ARRAY T2 OF
    ...
  ARRAY Tn OF T
```

Examples of array types:

```
ARRAY [0..N-1] OF CARDINAL
ARRAY [1..10], [1..20] OF [0..99]
ARRAY [-10.. + 10] OF BOOLEAN
ARRAY WeekDay OF Color
ARRAY Color OF WeekDay
```

6.5. Record types

A record type is a structure consisting of a fixed number of components of possibly different types. The record type declaration specifies for each component, called *field*, its type and an identifier which denotes the field. The scope of these field identifiers is the record definition itself, and they are also accessible within field designators (see 8.1) refering to components of record variables, and within with statements.

A record type may have several variant sections, in which case the first field of the section is called the *tag field*. Its value indicates which variant is assumed by the section. Individual variant structures are identified by *case labels*. These labels are constants of the type indicated by the tag field.

```
$  RecordType = RECORD FieldListSequence END.
$  FieldListSequence = FieldList {";" FieldList}.
$  FieldList = [IdentList ":" type |
$    CASE [ident ":"] qualident OF variant {"|" variant}
$    [ELSE FieldListSequence] END].
$  variant = CaseLabelList ":" FieldListSequence.
$  CaseLabelList = CaseLabels {"," CaseLabels}.
$  CaseLabels = ConstExpression [".." ConstExpression].
```

Examples of record types:

```
            RECORD day: [1..31];
                month: [1..12];
                year: [0..2000]
            END

            RECORD
                name,firstname: ARRAY [0..9] OF CHAR;
                age: [0..99];
                salary: REAL
            END

            RECORD x,y: T0;
                CASE tag0: Color OF
                    red:  a: Tr1; b: Tr2 |
                    green: c: Tg1; d: Tg2 |
                    blue:  e: Tb1; f: Tb2
                END;
                z: T0;
                CASE tag1: BOOLEAN OF
                    TRUE:  u,v: INTEGER |
                    FALSE: r,s: CARDINAL
                END
            END
```

The example above contains two variant sections. The variant of the first section is indicated by the value of the tag field tag0, the one of the second section by the tag field tag1.

6.6. Set types

A set type defined as SET OF T comprises all sets of values of its base type T. This must be a subrange of the integers between 0 and N-1, or a (subrange of an) enumeration type with at most N values, where N is a small constant determined by the implementation, usually the computer's wordsize or a small multiple thereof.

```
$  SetType = SET OF SimpleType.
```

The standard type BITSET is defined as follows, where W is a constant defined by the implementation, usually the word size of the computer.

```
            BITSET = SET OF [0 .. W-1]
```

148

6.7. Pointer types

Variables of a pointer type P assume as values pointers to variables of another type T. The pointer type P is said to be *bound* to T. A pointer value is generated by a call to the standard procedure NEW (see 10.2).

$ PointerType = POINTER TO type.

Besides such pointer values, a pointer variable may assume the value NIL, which can be thought as pointing to no variable at all.

6.8. Procedure types

Variables of a procedure type T may assume as their value a procedure P. The (types of the) formal parameters of P must be the same as those indicated in the formal type list of T. The same holds for the result type in the case of a function procedure.

Restriction: P must not be declared local to another procedure, and neither can it be a standard procedure.

$ ProcedureType = PROCEDURE [FormalTypeList].
$ FormalTypeList = "(" [[VAR] FormalType
$ {"," [VAR] FormalType}] ")" [":" qualident].

The standard type PROC denotes a parameterless procedure:

       PROC = PROCEDURE

7. Variable declarations

Variable declarations serve to introduce variables and associate them with a unique identifier and a fixed data type and structure. Variables whose identifiers appear in the same list all obtain the same type.

$ VariableDeclaration = IdentList ":" type.

The data type determines the set of values that a variable may assume and the operators that are applicable; it also defines the structure of the variable.

Examples of variable declarations (refer to examples in Ch. 6):

       i, j: CARDINAL
       k: INTEGER
       p, q: BOOLEAN
       s: BITSET
       F: Function
       a: ARRAY Index OF CARDINAL
       w: ARRAY [0..7] OF
                  RECORD ch : CHAR;
                    count : CARDINAL
                  END
       t: TreePtr

8. Expressions

Expressions are constructs denoting rules of computation for obtaining values of·variables and generating new values by the application of operators. Expressions consist of operands and operators. Parentheses may be used to express specific associations of operators and operands.

8.1. Operands

With the exception of literal constants, i.e. numbers, character strings, and sets (see Ch. 5), operands are denoted by *designators*. A designator consists of an identifier referring to the constant, variable, or procedure to be designated. This identifier may possibly be qualified by module identifiers (see Ch. 4 and 11), and it may be followed by selectors, if the designated object is an element of a structure. If the structure is an array A, then the designator A[E] denotes that component of A whose index is the current value of the expression E. The index type of A must be *assignment compatible* with the type of E (see 9.1). A designator of the form

A[E1, E2, ... , En]   stands for   A[E1][E2] ... [En].

If the structure is a record R, then the designator R.f denotes the record field f of R. The designator P↑ denotes the variable which is referenced by the pointer P.

$ designator = qualident {"." ident | "[" ExpList "]" | "↑"}.
$ ExpList = expression {"," expression}.

If the designated object is a variable, then the designator refers to the variable's current value. If the object is a function procedure, a designator without parameter list refers to that procedure. If it is followed by a (possibly empty) parameter list, the designator implies an activation of the procedure and stands for the value resulting from its execution, i.e. for the "returned" value. The (types of these) actual parameters must correspond to the formal parameters as specified in the procedure's declaration (see Ch. 10).

Examples of designators (see examples in Ch. 7):

k	(INTEGER)
a[i]	(CARDINAL)
w[3].ch	(CHAR)
t↑.key	(CARDINAL)
t↑.left↑.right	(TreePtr)

8.2. Operators

The syntax of expressions specifies operator precedences according to four classes of operators. The operator NOT has the highest precedence, followed by the so-called multiplying operators, then the so-called adding operators, and finally, with the lowest precedence, the relational operators. Sequences of operators of the same precedence are executed from left to right.

$ expression = SimpleExpression [relation SimpleExpression].
$ SimpleExpression = [" + "|"-"] term {AddOperator term}.
$ term = factor {MulOperator factor}.
$ factor = number | string | set | designator [ActualParameters] |
$ "(" expression ")" | NOT factor.
$ ActualParameters = "(" [ExpList] ")" .

The available operators are listed in the following tables. In some instances, several different operations are designated by the same operator symbol. In these cases, the actual operation is identified by the types of the operands.

8.2.1. Arithmetic operators

symbol	operation
+	addition
-	subtraction
*	multiplication
/	real division
DIV	integer division
MOD	modulus

These operators (except /) apply to operands of type INTEGER, CARDINAL, or subranges thereof. Both operands must be either of type CARDINAL or a subrange with base type CARDINAL, in which case the result is of type CARDINAL, or they must both be of type INTEGER or a subrange with base type INTEGER, in which case the result is of type INTEGER.

The operators +, -, and * also apply to operands of type REAL. In this case, both operands must be of type REAL, and the result is then also of type REAL. The division operator / applies to REAL operands only. When used as operators with a single operand only, - denotes sign inversion and + denotes the identity operation. Sign inversion applies to operands of type INTEGER or REAL. The operations DIV and MOD are defined by the following rules:

x DIV y is equal to the truncated quotient of x/y
x MOD y is equal to the remainder of the division x DIV y (for $y > 0$)
$x = (x$ DIV $y) * y + (x$ MOD $y)$

8.2.2. Logical operators

symbol	operation
OR	logical conjunction
AND	logical disjunction
NOT	negation

These operators apply to BOOLEAN operands and yield a BOOLEAN result.

p OR q   means   "if p then TRUE, otherwise q"
p AND q   means   "if p then q, otherwise FALSE"

8.2.3. Set operators

symbol	operation
+	set union
-	set difference
*	set intersection
/	symmetric set difference

These operations apply to operands of any set type and yield a result of the same type.

x IN $(s1 + s2)$ iff $(x$ IN $s1)$ OR $(x$ IN $s2)$
x IN $(s1 - s2)$ iff $(x$ IN $s1)$ AND NOT $(x$ IN $s2)$
x IN $(s1 * s2)$ iff $(x$ IN $s1)$ AND $(x$ IN $s2)$
x IN $(s1 / s2)$ iff $(x$ IN $s1)$ # $(x$ IN $s2)$

8.2.4. Relations

Relations yield a BOOLEAN result. The ordering relations apply to the basic types INTEGER, CARDINAL, BOOLEAN, CHAR, REAL, to enumerations, and to subrange types.

symbol	relation
=	equal
#	unequal
<	less
<=	less or equal (set inclusion)
>	greater
>=	greater or equal (set inclusion)
IN	contained in (set membership)

The relations = and # also apply to sets and pointers. If applied to sets, <= and >= denote (improper) inclusion. The relation IN denotes set membership. In an expression of the form x IN s, the expression s must be of type SET OF T, where T is (compatible with) the type of x.

Examples of expressions (refer to examples in Ch. 7):

1980	(CARDINAL)
k DIV 3	(INTEGER)
NOT p OR q	(BOOLEAN)
(i + j) * (i-j)	(CARDINAL)
s - {8,9,13}	(BITSET)
a[i] + a[j]	(CARDINAL)
a[i + j] * a[i-j]	(CARDINAL)
(0<= k) & (k<100)	(BOOLEAN)
t↑.key = 0	(BOOLEAN)
{13..15} <= s	(BOOLEAN)
i IN {0, 5..8, 15}	(BOOLEAN)

9. Statements

Statements denote actions. There are elementary and structured statements. Elementary statements are not composed of any parts that are themselves statements. They are the assignment, the procedure call, and the return and exit statements. Structured statements are composed of parts that are themselves statements. These are used to express sequencing, and conditional, selective, and repetitive execution.

```
$  statement = [assignment | ProcedureCall |
$     IfStatement | CaseStatement | WhileStatement |
$     RepeatStatement | LoopStatement | ForStatement |
$     WithStatement | EXIT | RETURN [expression] ].
```

A statement may also be empty, in which case it denotes no action. The empty statement is included in order to relax punctuation rules in statement sequences.

9.1. Assignments

The assignment serves to replace the current value of a variable by a new value indicated by an expression. The assignment operator is written as ":=" and pronounced as "becomes".

```
$  assignment = designator ":=" expression.
```

152

The designator to the left of the assignment operator denotes a variable. After an assignment is executed, the variable has the value obtained by evaluating the expression. The old value is lost (overwritten). The type of the variable must be assignment compatible with the type of the expression. Operand types are said to be *assignment compatible,* if either they are compatible or both are INTEGER or CARDINAL or subranges with base types INTEGER or CARDINAL.

A string of length n1 can be assigned to a string variable of length n2 > n1. In this case, the string value is extended with a null character (0C).

Examples of assignments:

```
i := k
p := i = j
j := log2(i + j)
F := log2
s := {2,3,5,7,11,13}
a[i] := (i + j) * (i-j)
t↑.key := i
w[i + 1].ch := "A"
```

9.2. Procedure calls

A procedure call serves to activate a procedure. The procedure call may contain a list of actual parameters which are substituted in place of their corresponding formal parameters defined in the procedure declaration (see Ch. 10). The correspondence is established by the positions of the parameters in the lists of actual and formal parameters respectively. There exist two kinds of parameters: *variable* and *value parameters.*

In the case of variable parameters, the actual parameter must be a designator denoting a variable. If it designates a component of a structured variable, the selector is evaluated when the formal/actual parameter substitution takes place, i.e. before the execution of the procedure. If the parameter is a value parameter, the corresponding actual parameter must be an expression. This expression is evaluated prior to the procedure activation, and the resulting value is assigned to the formal parameter which now constitutes a local variable. The types of corresponding actual and formal parameters must be compatible in the case of variable parameters and assignment compatible in the case of value parameters.

$ ProcedureCall = designator [ActualParameters].

Examples of procedure calls:

```
Read(i)          (see Ch. 10)
Write(j*2 + 1,6)
INC(a[i])
```

9.3. Statement sequences

Statement sequences denote the sequence of actions specified by the component statements which are separated by semicolons.

$ StatementSequence = statement {";" statement}.

9.4. If statements

$ IfStatement = IF expression THEN StatementSequence
$ {ELSIF expression THEN StatementSequence}

```
$    [ELSE StatementSequence] END.
```

The expressions following the symbols IF and ELSIF are of type BOOLEAN. They are evaluated in the sequence of their occurrence, until one yields the value TRUE. Then its associated statement sequence is executed. If an ELSE clause is present, its associated statement sequence is executed if and only if all Boolean expressions yielded the value FALSE.

Example:

```
IF (ch >= "A") & (ch <= "Z") THEN ReadIdentifier
ELSIF (ch >= "0") & (ch <= "9") THEN ReadNumber
ELSIF ch = '"' THEN ReadString('"')
ELSIF ch = "'" THEN ReadString("'")
ELSE SpecialCharacter
END
```

9.5. Case statements

Case statements specify the selection and execution of a statement sequence according to the value of an expression. First the case expression is evaluated, then the statement sequence is executed whose case label list contains the obtained value. The type of the case expression must be a basic type (except REAL), an enumeration type, or a subrange type, and all labels must be compatible with that type. Case labels are constants, and no value must occur more than once. If the value of the expression does not occur as a label of any case, the statement sequence following the symbol ELSE is selected.

```
$  CaseStatement = CASE expression OF case {"|" case}
$    [ELSE StatementSequence] END.
$  case = CaseLabelList ":" StatementSequence.
```

Example:

```
CASE i OF
   0: p := p OR q; x := x+y |
   1: p := p OR q; x := x-y |
   2: p := p AND q; x := x*y
END
```

9.6. While statements

While statements specify the repeated execution of a statement sequence depending on the value of a Boolean expression. The expression is evaluated before each subsequent execution of the statement sequence. The repetition stops as soon as this evaluation yields the value FALSE.

```
$  WhileStatement = WHILE expression DO StatementSequence END.
```

Examples:

```
WHILE j > 0 DO
   j := j DIV 2; i := i+1
END

WHILE i # j DO
   IF i > j THEN i := i-j
   ELSE j := j-i
```

```
        END
    END

    WHILE (t # NIL) & (t↑.key # i) DO
        t := t↑.left
    END
```

9.7. Repeat statements

Repeat statements specify the repeated execution of a statement sequence depending on the value of a Boolean expression. The expression is evaluated after each execution of the statement sequence, and the repetition stops as soon as it yields the value TRUE. Hence, the statement sequence is executed at least once.

$ RepeatStatement = REPEAT StatementSequence UNTIL expression.

Example:

```
        REPEAT k := i MOD j; i := j; j := k
        UNTIL j = 0
```

9.8. For statements

The for statement indicates that a statement sequence is to be repeatedly executed while a progression of values is assigned to a variable. This variable is called the *control variable* of the for statement. It cannot be a component of a structured variable, it cannot be imported, nor can it be a parameter. Its value should not be changed by the statement sequence.

$ ForStatement = FOR ident ":=" expression TO expression
$ [BY ConstExpression] DO StatementSequence END.

The for statement

```
    FOR v := A TO B BY C DO SS END
```

expresses repeated execution of the statement sequence SS with v successively assuming the values A, $A+C$, $A+2C$, ... , $A+nC$, where $A+nC$ is the last term not exceeding B. v is called the control variable, A the starting value, B the limit, and C the increment. A and B must be assignment compatible with v; C must be a constant of type INTEGER or CARDINAL. If no increment is specified, it is assumed to be 1.

Examples:

```
        FOR i := 1 TO 80 DO j := j + a[i]  END
        FOR i := 80 TO 2 BY -1 DO a[i] := a[i-1] END
```

9.9. Loop statements

A loop statement specifies the repeated execution of a statement sequence. It is terminated by the execution of any exit statement within that sequence.

$ LoopStatement = LOOP StatementSequence END.

Example:

```
        LOOP
        IF t1↑.key > x THEN t2 := t1↑.left; p := TRUE
        ELSE t2 := t1↑.right; p := FALSE
        END ;
```

```
    IF t2 = NIL THEN
      EXIT
    END ;
    t1 : = t2
  END
```

While, repeat, and for statements can be expressed by loop statements containing a single exit statement. Their use is recommended as they characterize the most frequently occurring situations where termination depends either on a single condition at either the beginning or end of the repeated statement sequence, or on reaching the limit of an arithmetic progression. The loop statement is, however, necessary to express the continuous repetition of cyclic processes, where no termination is specified. It is also useful to express situations exemplified above. Exit statements are contextually, although not syntactically bound to the loop statement which contains them.

9.10. With statements

The with statement specifies a record variable and a statement sequence. In these statements the qualification of field identifiers may be omitted, if they are to refer to the variable specified in the with clause. If the designator denotes a component of a structured variable, the selector is evaluated once (before the statement sequence). The with statement opens a new scope.

$ WithStatement = WITH designator DO StatementSequence END .

Example:

```
    WITH t↑ DO
      key : = 0; left : = NIL; right : = NIL
    END
```

9.11. Return and exit statements

A return statement consists of the symbol RETURN, possibly followed by an expression. It indicates the termination of a procedure (or a module body), and the expression specifies the value returned as result of a function procedure. Its type must be assignment compatible with the result type specified in the procedure heading (see Ch. 10).

Function procedures require the presence of a return statement indicating the result value. There may be several, although only one will be executed. In proper procedures, a return statement is implied by the end of the procedure body. An explicit return statement therefore appears as an additional, probably exceptional termination point.

An exit statement consists of the symbol EXIT, and it specifies termination of the enclosing loop statement and continuation with the statement following that loop statement (see 9.9).

10. Procedure declarations

Procedure declarations consist of a *procedure heading* and a block which is said to be the *procedure body*. The heading specifies the procedure identifier and the *formal parameters*. The block contains declarations and statements. The procedure identifier is repeated at the end of the procedure declaration.

There are two kinds of procedures, namely *proper procedures* and *function procedures*. The latter are activated by a function designator as a constituent of an expression, and yield a result that is an operand in the expression. Proper procedures are activated by a procedure call. The function procedure is distinguished in the declaration by indication of the type of its result following the parameter list. Its body must contain a RETURN statement which defines the result of the function procedure.

All constants, variables, types, modules and procedures declared within the block that constitutes the procedure body are *local* to the procedure. The values of local variables, including those defined within a local module, are undefined upon entry to the procedure. Since procedures may be declared as local objects too, procedure declarations may be nested. Every object is said to be declared at a certain *level* of nesting. If it is declared local to a procedure at level k, it has itself level k+1. Objects declared in the module that constitutes a compilation unit (see Ch. 14) are defined to be at level 0.

In addition to its formal parameters and local objects, also the objects declared in the environment of the procedure are known and accessible in the procedure (with the exception of those objects that have the same name as objects declared locally).

The use of the procedure identifier in a call within its declaration implies recursive activation of the procedure.

$ ProcedureDeclaration = ProcedureHeading ";" block ident.
$ ProcedureHeading = PROCEDURE ident [FormalParameters].
$ block = {declaration} [BEGIN StatementSequence] END.
$ declaration = CONST {ConstantDeclaration ";"} |
$ TYPE {TypeDeclaration ";"} |
$ VAR {VariableDeclaration ";"} |
$ ProcedureDeclaration ";" | ModuleDeclaration ";".

10.1. Formal parameters

Formal parameters are identifiers which denote actual parameters specified in the procedure call. The correspondence between formal and actual parameters is established when the procedure is called. There are two kinds of parameters, namely *value* and *variable parameters*. The kind is indicated in the formal parameter list. Value parameters stand for local variables to which the result of the evaluation of the corresponding actual parameter is assigned as initial value. Variable parameters correspond to actual parameters that are variables, and they stand for these variables. Variable parameters are indicated by the symbol VAR, value parameters by the absence of the symbol VAR.

Formal parameters are local to the procedure, i.e. their scope is the program text which constitutes the procedure declaration.

$ FormalParameters =
$ "(" [FPSection {";" FPSection}] ")" [":" qualident].
$ FPSection = [VAR] IdentList ":" FormalType.
$ FormalType = [ARRAY OF] qualident.

The type of each formal parameter is specified in the parameter list. In the case of variable parameters it must be compatible with its corresponding actual parameter (see 9.2), in the case of value parameters the formal type must be assignment compatible with the actual type (see 9.1). If the parameter is an array, the form

    ARRAY OF T

may be used, where the specification of the actual index bounds is omitted. The parameter is then said to be an *open array parameter*. T must be the same as the element type of the actual array, and the index range is mapped onto the integers 0 to N-1, where N is the number of elements. The formal array can be accessed elementwise only, or it may occur as actual parameter whose formal parameter is without specified index bounds. A function procedure without parameters has an empty parameter list. It must be called by a function designator whose actual parameter list is empty too.

Restriction: If a formal parameter specifies a procedure type, then the corresponding actual parameter must be either a procedure declared at level 0 or a variable (or parameter) of that procedure type. It cannot be a standard procedure.

Examples of procedure declarations:

```
      PROCEDURE Read(VAR x: CARDINAL);
        VAR i : CARDINAL; ch: CHAR;
      BEGIN i : = 0;
        REPEAT ReadChar(ch)
        UNTIL (ch > = "0") & (ch < = "9");
        REPEAT i : = 10*i + (ORD(ch)-ORD("0"));
          ReadChar(ch)
        UNTIL (ch < "0") OR (ch > "9");
        x : = i
      END Read

      PROCEDURE Write(x,n: CARDINAL);
        VAR i: CARDINAL;
          buf: ARRAY [1..10] OF CARDINAL;
      BEGIN i : = 0;
        REPEAT INC(i); buf[i] : = x MOD 10; x : = x DIV 10
        UNTIL x = 0;
        WHILE n > i DO
          WriteChar(" "); DEC(n)
        END ;
        REPEAT WriteChar(CHR(buf[i] + ORD("0")));
          DEC(i)
        UNTIL i = 0;
        END Write

      PROCEDURE log2(x: CARDINAL): CARDINAL;
        VAR y: CARDINAL;  (*assume x>0*)
      BEGIN x : = x-1; y : = 0;
        WHILE x > 0 DO
          x : = x DIV 2; y : = y + 1
        END ;
        RETURN y
      END log2
```

10.2. Standard procedures

Standard procedures are predefined. Some are *generic* procedures that cannot be explicitly declared, i.e. they apply to classes of operand types or have several possible parameter list forms. Standard procedures are

ABS(x)   absolute value; result type = argument type.

CAP(ch)   if ch is a lower case letter, the corresponding capital letter;
                 if ch is a capital letter, the same letter.

CHR(x)	the character with ordinal number x. CHR(x) = VAL(CHAR,x)
FLOAT(x)	x of type CARDINAL represented as a value of type REAL.
HIGH(a)	high index bound of array a.
ODD(x)	x MOD 2 # 0.
ORD(x)	ordinal number (of type CARDINAL) of x in the set of values defined by type T of x. T is any enumeration type, CHAR, INTEGER, or CARDINAL.
TRUNC(x)	real number x truncated to its integral part (of type CARDINAL).
VAL(T,x)	the value with ordinal number x and with type T. T is any enumeration type, CHAR, INTEGER, or CARDINAL. VAL(T,ORD(x)) = x , if x of type T.

DEC(x)	x := x-1
DEC(x,n)	x := x-n
EXCL(s,i)	s := s - {i}
HALT	terminate program execution
INC(x)	x := x+1
INC(x,n)	x := x+n
INCL(s,i)	s := s + {i}

The procedures INC and DEC also apply to operands x of enumeration types and of type CHAR. In these cases they replace x by its (n-th) successor or predecessor.

NEW and DISPOSE are translated into calls to ALLOCATE and DEALLOCATE, procedures that are either explicitly programmed or imported from another module.

NEW(p)	=	ALLOCATE(p,TSIZE(T))
DISPOSE(p)	=	DEALLOCATE(p,TSIZE(T))
NEW(p,t1,t2, ...)	=	ALLOCATE(p,TSIZE(T,t1,t2,...))
DISPOSE(p,t1,t2, ...)	=	DEALLOCATE(p,TSIZE(T,t1,t2,...))

TSIZE is defined in Chapter 12, and p is declared as "VAR p: POINTER TO T". These procedures must be compatible with the type

    PROCEDURE (VAR ADDRESS, CARDINAL)

11. Modules

A module constitutes a collection of declarations and a sequence of statements. They are enclosed in the brackets MODULE and END. The module heading contains the module identifier, and possibly a number of *import lists* and an *export list.* The former specify all identifiers of objects that are declared outside but used within the module and therefore have to be imported. The export-list specifies all identifiers of objects declared within the module and used outside. Hence, a module constitutes a wall around its local objects whose transparency is strictly under control of the programmer.

Objects local to a module are said to be at the same scope level as the module. They can be considered as being local to the procedure enclosing the module but residing within a more restricted scope.

$ ModuleDeclaration =

```
$   MODULE ident [priority] ";" {import} [export] block ident.
$   priority = "[" ConstExpression "]".
$   export = EXPORT [QUALIFIED] IdentList ";".
$   import = [FROM ident] IMPORT IdentList ";".
```

The module identifier is repeated at the end of the declaration.

The statement sequence that constitutes the *module body* is executed when the procedure to which the module is local is called. If several modules are declared, then these bodies are executed in the sequence in which the modules occur. These bodies serve to initialize local variables and must be considered as prefixes to the enclosing procedure's statement part.

If an identifier occurs in the import (export) list, then the denoted object may be used inside (outside) the module as if the module brackets did not exist. If, however, the symbol EXPORT is followed by the symbol QUALIFIED, then the listed identifiers must be prefixed with the module's identifier when used outside the module. This case is called *qualified export,* and is used when modules are designed which are to be used in coexistence with other modules not known a priori. Qualified export serves to avoid clashes of identical identifiers exported from different modules (and presumably denoting different objects).

A module may feature several import lists which may be prefixed with the symbol FROM and a module identifier. The FROM clause has the effect of unqualifying the imported identifiers. Hence they may be used within the module as if they had been exported in normal, i.e. non-qualified mode.

If a record type is exported, all its field identifiers are exported too. The same holds for the constant identifiers in the case of an enumeration type. If a module identifier is exported, then all identifiers occurring in that module's export list are also exported.

Standard identifiers are always imported automatically. As a consequence, standard identifiers can be redeclared in procedures only, but not in modules, including the compilation unit (see Ch. 14).

Examples of module declarations:

The following module serves to scan a text and to copy it into an output character sequence. Input is obtained characterwise by a procedure inchr and delivered by a procedure outchr. The characters are given in the ASCII code; control characters are ignored, with the exception of LF (line feed) and FS (file separator). They are both translated into a blank and cause the Boolean variables eoln (end of line) and eof (end of file) to be set respectively. FS is assumed to be preceded by LF.

```
MODULE LineInput;
 IMPORT inchr, outchr;
 EXPORT read, NewLine, NewFile, eoln, eof, lno;
 CONST LF = 12C; CR = 15C; FS = 34C;

 VAR lno: CARDINAL; (*line number*)
   ch: CHAR;   (*last character read*)
   eof, eoln: BOOLEAN;

 PROCEDURE NewFile;
 BEGIN
  IF NOT eof THEN
    REPEAT inchr(ch) UNTIL ch = FS;
```

```
    END;
     eof : = FALSE; eoln : = FALSE; lno : = 0
   END NewFile;

   PROCEDURE NewLine;
   BEGIN
     IF NOT eoln THEN
     REPEAT inchr(ch) UNTIL ch = LF;
       outchr(CR); outchr(LF)
     END ;
     eoln : = FALSE; INC(lno)
   END NewLine;

   PROCEDURE read(VAR x: CHAR);
   BEGIN (*assume NOT eoln AND NOT eof*)
     LOOP inchr(ch); outchr(ch);
      IF ch >= " " THEN
        x : = ch; EXIT
      ELSIF ch = LF THEN
        x : = " "; eoln : = TRUE; EXIT
      ELSIF ch = FS THEN
        x : = " "; eoln : = TRUE; eof : = TRUE; EXIT
      END
     END
   END read;

   BEGIN eof : = TRUE; eoln : = TRUE
   END LineInput
```

The next example is a module which operates a disk track reservation table, and protects it from unauthorized access. A function procedure NewTrack yields the number of a free track which is becoming reserved. Tracks can be released by calling procedure ReturnTrack.

```
   MODULE TrackReservation;
   EXPORT NewTrack, ReturnTrack;
   CONST ntr = 1024;  (* no. of tracks *)
     w = 16;      (* word size *)
     m = ntr DIV w;

   VAR i: CARDINAL;
     free: ARRAY [0..m-1] OF BITSET;

   PROCEDURE NewTrack(): INTEGER;
     (*reserves a new track and yields its index as result,
      if a free track is found, and -1 otherwise*)
     VAR i,j: CARDINAL; found: BOOLEAN;
   BEGIN found : = FALSE; i : = m;
     REPEAT DEC(i); j : = w;
      REPEAT DEC(j);
        IF j IN free[i] THEN found: = TRUE END
```

```
        UNTIL found OR (j = 0)
        UNTIL found OR (i = 0);
        IF found THEN EXCL(free[i],j); RETURN i*w + j
        ELSE RETURN -1
        END
    END NewTrack;

    PROCEDURE ReturnTrack(k: CARDINAL);
    BEGIN (*assume 0 < = k < ntr *)
        INCL(free[k DIV w], k MOD w)
    END ReturnTrack;

    BEGIN (*mark all tracks free*)
        FOR i : = 0 TO m-1 DO free[i] : = {0..w-1} END
    END TrackReservation
```

12. System-dependent facilities

Modula-2 offers certain facilities that are necessary to program *low-level* operations referring directly to objects particular of a given computer and/or implementation. These include for example facilities for accessing devices that are controlled by the computer, and facilities to break the data type compatibility rules otherwise imposed by the language definition. Such facilities are to be used with utmost care, and it is strongly recommended to restrict their use to specific modules (called low-level modules). Most of them appear in the form of data types and procedures imported from the standard module SYSTEM. A low-level module is therefore explicitly characterized by the identifier SYSTEM appearing in its import list.

Note: Because the objects imported from SYSTEM obey special rules, this module must be known to the compiler. It is therefore called a pseudo-module and need not be supplied as a separate definition module (see Ch. 14).

The module SYSTEM exports the types WORD, ADDRESS, PROCESS, and the procedures ADR, SIZE, TSIZE, NEWPROCESS, TRANSFER, and possibly other identifiers depending on the implementation being used (see Ch. 13).

The type WORD represents an individually accessible storage unit. No operation except assignment is defined on this type. However, if a formal parameter of a procedure is of type WORD, the corresponding actual parameter may be of any type that uses one storage word in the given implementation. This includes the types CARDINAL, INTEGER, BITSET and all pointers. If a formal parameter has the type ARRAY OF WORD, its corresponding actual parameter may be of any type; in particular it may be a record type to be interpreted as an array of words.

The type ADDRESS is defined as

        ADDRESS = POINTER TO WORD

It is compatible with all pointer types, and also with the type CARDINAL. Therefore, all operators for integer arithmetic apply to operands of this type. Hence, the type ADDRESS can be used to perform address computations and to export the results as pointers. The following example of a primitive storage allocator demonstrates a typical usage of the type ADDRESS.

```
    MODULE Storage;
      FROM SYSTEM IMPORT ADDRESS;
```

162

```
        EXPORT Allocate;

        VAR lastused: ADDRESS;

        PROCEDURE Allocate (VAR a: ADDRESS; n: CARDINAL);
        BEGIN a : = lastused;  INC(lastused, n)
        END Allocate;

        BEGIN lastused : = 0
        END Storage
```

The function ADR(x) denotes the storage address of the variable x and is of type
ADDRESS. SIZE(x) denotes the number of storage units assigned to the variable x.
TSIZE(T) is the number of storage units assigned to any variable of type T. SIZE and
TSIZE are of type CARDINAL.

Examples:

        ADR(lastused)   SIZE(a)   TSIZE(Node)

Besides those exported from the pseudo-module SYSTEM, there are two other facilities
whose characteristics are system-dependent. The first is the possibility to use a type
identifier T as a name denoting the *type transfer function* from the type of the operand to the
type T. Evidently, such functions are data representation dependent, and they involve no
explicit conversion instructions.

The second facility is used in variable declarations. It allows to specify the absolute address
of a variable and to override the allocation scheme of a compiler. This facility is intended
for access to storage locations with specific purpose and fixed address, such as e.g. device
registers on computers with "memory-mapped I/O". This address is specified as a constant
integer expression enclosed in brackets immediately following the identifier in the variable
declaration. The choice of an appropriate data type is left to the programmer. For
examples, refer to 13.2.

13. Processes

Modula-2 is designed primarily for implementation on a conventional single-processor
computer. For multiprogramming it offers only some basic facilities which allow the
specification of quasi-concurrent processes and of genuine concurrency for peripheral
devices. The word *process* is here used with the meaning of *coroutine.* Coroutines are
processes that are executed by a (single) processor one at a time.

13.1. Creating a process and transfer of control

A new process is created by a call to

PROCEDURE NEWPROCESS(P: PROC; A: ADDRESS; n: CARDINAL; VAR p1: PROCESS)

        P   denotes the procedure which constitutes the process,
        A   is the base address of the process' workspace,
        n   is the size of this workspace,
        p1 is the result parameter.

A new process with P as program and A as workspace of size n is assigned to p1. This
process is allocated, but not activated. P must be a parameterless procedure declared at

level 0.

A transfer of control between two processes is specified by a call to

PROCEDURE TRANSFER(VAR p1, p2: PROCESS)

This call suspends the current process, assigns it to p1, and resumes the process designated by p2. Evidently, p2 must have been assigned a process by an earlier call to either NEWPROCESS or TRANSFER. Both procedures, as well as the type PROCESS, must be imported from the module SYSTEM. A program terminates, when control reaches the end of a procedure which is the body of a process.

Note: assignment to p1 occurs after identification of the new process p2; hence, the actual parameters may be identical.

13.2. Device processes and interrupts

If a process contains an operation of a peripheral device, then the processor may be transferred to another process after the operation of the device has been initiated, thereby leading to a concurrent execution of that other process with the *device process*. Usually, termination of the device's operation is signalled by an interrupt of the main processor. In terms of Modula-2, an interrupt is a transfer operation. This interrupt transfer is (in Modula-2 implemented on the PDP-11) preprogrammed by and combined with the transfer after device initiation. This combination is expressed by a call to

PROCEDURE IOTRANSFER(VAR p1, p2: PROCESS; va: CARDINAL)

In analogy to TRANSFER, this call suspends the calling device process, assigns it to p1, resumes (transfers to) the suspended process p2, and in addition causes the interrupt transfer occurring upon device completion to assign the interrupted process to p2 and to resume the device process p1. va is the interrupt vector address assigned to the device. The procedure IOTRANSFER must be imported from the module SYSTEM, and should be considered as PDP-11 implementation-specific.

It is necessary that interrupts can be postponed (disabled) at certain times, e.g. when variables common to the cooperating processes are accessed, or when other, possibly time-critical operations have priority. Therefore, every module is given a certain priority level, and every device capable of interrupting is given a priority level. Execution of a program can be interrupted, if and only if the interrupting device has a priority that is greater than the priority level of the module containing the statement currently being executed. Whereas the device priority is defined by the hardware, the priority level of each module is specified by its heading. If an explicit specification is absent, the level in any procedure is that of the calling program. IOTRANSFER must be used within modules with a specified priority only.

The following example (programmed for the PDP-11) shows a module with a process that acts as a driver for a typewriter. The module contains a buffer B for N characters.

```
MODULE Typewriter [4]; (*typewriter interrupt priority = 4*)
  FROM SYSTEM IMPORT
    PROCESS, NEWPROCESS, TRANSFER, IOTRANSFER, LISTEN,
    WORD, ADR, SIZE;
  EXPORT typeout;

  CONST N = 32;
```

```
      VAR n: INTEGER;    (*no. of chars in buffer*)
        in, out: [1..N];
        B: ARRAY [1..N] OF CHAR;
        PRO: PROCESS; (*producer*)
        CON: PROCESS; (*consumer = typewriter driver*)
        wsp: ARRAY [1..50] OF WORD;
        TWS [177564B]: BITSET;   (*status register*)
        TWB [177566B]: CHAR;     (*buffer register*)

      PROCEDURE typeout(ch: CHAR);
      BEGIN INC(n);
        WHILE n > N DO LISTEN END ;
        B[in] : = ch; in : = in MOD N + 1;
        IF n = 0 THEN TRANSFER(PRO,CON) END
      END typeout;

      PROCEDURE driver;
      BEGIN
        LOOP DEC(n);
          IF n < 0 THEN TRANSFER(CON,PRO) END ;
          TWB : = B[out]; out : = out MOD N + 1;
          TWS : = {6}; IOTRANSFER(CON,PRO,64B); TWS : = {}
        END
      END driver;

      BEGIN n : = 0; in : = 1; out : = 1;
        NEWPROCESS(driver, ADR(wsp), SIZE(wsp), CON);
        TRANSFER(PRO,CON)
      END Typewriter
```

LISTEN must be a procedure that lowers the processor's priority level so that pending interrupts may be accepted.

14. Compilation units

A text which is accepted by the compiler as a unit is called a *compilation unit*. There are three kinds of compilation units: main modules, definition modules, and implementation modules. A main module constitutes a main program and consists of a so-called *program module*. In particular, it has no export list. Imported objects are defined in other (separately compiled) program parts which themselves are subdivided into two units, called definition module and implementation module.

The *definition module* specifies the names and properties of objects that are relevant to clients, i.e. other modules which import from it. The *implementation module* contains local objects and statements that need not be known to a client. In particular the definition module contains the export list, constant, type, and variable declarations, and specifications of procedure headings. The corresponding implementation module contains the complete procedure declarations, and possibly further declarations of objects not exported. Definition and implementation modules exist in pairs. Both may contain import lists, and all objects declared in the definition module are available in the corresponding implementation module without explicit import.

$ DefinitionModule = DEFINITION MODULE ident ";" {import}

$ [export] {definition} END ident ".".
$ definition = CONST {ConstantDeclaration ";"} |
$ TYPE {ident [" = " type] ";"} |
$ VAR {VariableDeclaration ";"} |
$ ProcedureHeading ";".
$ ProgramModule = MODULE ident [priority] ";" {import} block ident ".".
$ CompilationUnit = DefinitionModule | [IMPLEMENTATION] ProgramModule .

The definition module evidently represents the interface between the definition/implementation module pair on one side and its clients on the other side.

Definition modules require the use of qualified export. Type definitions may consist of the full specification of the type (in this case its export is said to be transparent), or they may consist of the type identifier only. In this case the full specification must appear in the corresponding implementation module, and its export is said to be *opaque*. The type is known in the importing client modules by its name only, and all its properties are hidden. Therefore, procedures operating on operands of this type, and in particular operating on its components, must be defined in the same implementation module which hides the type's properties. Opaque export is restricted to pointers and to subranges of standard types.

Appendix 1

The Syntax of Modula-2

```
1   ident = letter {letter | digit}.
2   number = integer | real.
3   integer = digit {digit} | octalDigit {octalDigit} ("B"|"C")|
4      digit {hexDigit} "H".
5   real = digit {digit} "." {digit} [ScaleFactor].
6   ScaleFactor = "E" [" + "|"-"] digit {digit}.
7   hexDigit = digit |"A"|"B"|"C"|"D"|"E"|"F".
8   digit = octalDigit | "8"|"9".
9   octalDigit = "0"|"1"|"2"|"3"|"4"|"5"|"6"|"7".
10  string = "'" {character} "'" | '"' {character} '"' .
11  qualident = ident {"." ident}.
12  ConstantDeclaration = ident " = " ConstExpression.
13  ConstExpression = SimpleConstExpr [relation SimpleConstExpr].
14  relation = " = " | " # " | "<>" | "<" | "< = " | ">" | "> = " | IN .
15  SimpleConstExpr = [" + "|"-"] ConstTerm {AddOperator ConstTerm}.
16  AddOperator = " + " | "-" | OR .
17  ConstTerm = ConstFactor {MulOperator ConstFactor}.
18  MulOperator = "*" | "/" | DIV | MOD | AND | "&" .
19  ConstFactor = qualident | number | string | set |
20     "(" ConstExpression ")" | NOT ConstFactor.
21  set = [qualident] "{" [element {"," element}] "}".
22  element = ConstExpression [".." ConstExpression].
23  TypeDeclaration = ident " = " type.
24  type = SimpleType | ArrayType | RecordType | SetType |
25     PointerType | ProcedureType.
26  SimpleType = qualident | enumeration | SubrangeType.
27  enumeration = "(" IdentList ")".
28  IdentList = ident {"," ident}.
29  SubrangeType = "[" ConstExpression ".." ConstExpression "]".
30  ArrayType = ARRAY SimpleType {"," SimpleType} OF type.
31  RecordType = RECORD FieldListSequence END.
32  FieldListSequence = FieldList {";" FieldList}.
33  FieldList = [IdentList ":" type |
34     CASE [ident ":"] qualident OF variant {"|" variant}
35     [ELSE FieldListSequence] END].
36  variant = CaseLabelList ":" FieldListSequence.
37  CaseLabelList = CaseLabels {"," CaseLabels}.
38  CaseLabels = ConstExpression [".." ConstExpression].
39  SetType = SET OF SimpleType.
40  PointerType = POINTER TO type.
41  ProcedureType = PROCEDURE [FormalTypeList].
42  FormalTypeList = "(" [[VAR] FormalType
43     {"," [VAR] FormalType} ")" [":" qualident].
44  VariableDeclaration = IdentList ":" type.
```

```
45   designator = qualident {"." ident | "[" ExpList "]" | "↑"}.
46   ExpList = expression {"," expression}.
47   expression = SimpleExpression [relation SimpleExpression].
48   SimpleExpression = [" + "|"-"] term {AddOperator term}.
49   term = factor {MulOperator factor}.
50   factor = number | string | set | designator [ActualParameters] |
51      "(" expression ")" | NOT factor.
52   ActualParameters = "(" [ExpList] ")" .
53   statement = [assignment | ProcedureCall |
54      IfStatement | CaseStatement | WhileStatement |
55      RepeatStatement | LoopStatement | ForStatement |
56      WithStatement | EXIT | RETURN [expression] ].
57   assignment = designator ": = " expression.
58   ProcedureCall = designator [ActualParameters].
59   StatementSequence = statement {";" statement}.
60   IfStatement = IF expression THEN StatementSequence
61      {ELSIF expression THEN StatementSequence}
62      [ELSE StatementSequence] END.
63   CaseStatement = CASE expression OF case {"|" case}
64      [ELSE StatementSequence] END.
65   case = CaseLabelList ":" StatementSequence.
66   WhileStatement = WHILE expression DO StatementSequence END.
67   RepeatStatement = REPEAT StatementSequence UNTIL expression.
68   ForStatement = FOR ident ": = " expression TO expression
69      [BY ConstExpression] DO StatementSequence END.
70   LoopStatement = LOOP StatementSequence END.
71   WithStatement = WITH designator DO StatementSequence END .
72   ProcedureDeclaration = ProcedureHeading ";" block ident.
73   ProcedureHeading = PROCEDURE ident [FormalParameters].
74   block = {declaration} [BEGIN StatementSequence] END.
75   declaration = CONST {ConstantDeclaration ";"} |
76      TYPE {TypeDeclaration ";"} |
77      VAR {VariableDeclaration ";"} |
78      ProcedureDeclaration ";" | ModuleDeclaration ";".
79   FormalParameters =
80      "(" [FPSection {";" FPSection}] ")" [":" qualident].
81   FPSection = [VAR] IdentList ":" FormalType.
82   FormalType = [ARRAY OF] qualident.
83   ModuleDeclaration =
84      MODULE ident [priority] ";" {import} [export] block ident.
85   priority = "[" ConstExpression "]".
86   export = EXPORT [QUALIFIED] IdentList ";".
87   import = [FROM ident] IMPORT IdentList ";".
88   DefinitionModule = DEFINITION MODULE ident ";" {import}
89      [export] {definition} END ident ".".
90   definition = CONST {ConstantDeclaration ";"} |
91      TYPE {ident [" = " type] ";"} |
92      VAR {VariableDeclaration ";"} |
93      ProcedureHeading ";" .
94   ProgramModule =
95      MODULE ident [priority] ";" {import} block ident ".." .
```

96 CompilationUnit = DefinitionModule |
97   [IMPLEMENTATION] ProgramModule.

ActualParameters	58	-52	50						
AddOperator	48	-16	15						
ArrayType	-30	24							
assignment	-57	53							
block	95	84	-74	72					
case	-65	63	63						
CaseLabelList	65	-37	36						
CaseLabels	-38	37	37						
CaseStatement	-63	54							
character	10	10							
CompilationUnit	-96								
ConstantDeclaration	90	75	-12						
ConstExpression	85	69	38	38	29	29	22	22	20
	-13	12							
ConstFactor	20	-19	17	17					
ConstTerm	-17	15	15						
declaration	-75	74							
definition	-90	89							
DefinitionModule	96	-88							
designator	71	58	57	50	-45				
digit	-8	7	6	6	5	5	5	4	3
	3	1							
element	-22	21	21						
enumeration	-27	26							
ExpList	52	-46	45						
export	89	-86	84						
expression	68	68	67	66	63	61	60	57	56
	51	-47	46	46					
factor	51	-50	49	49					
FieldList	-33	32	32						
FieldListSequence	36	35	-32	31					
FormalParameters	-79	73							
FormalType	-82	81	43	42					
FormalTypeList	-42	41							
ForStatement	-68	55							
FPSection	-81	80	80						
hexDigit	-7	4							
ident	95	95	91	89	88	87	84	84	73
	72	68	45	34	28	28	23	12	11
	11	-1							
IdentList	87	86	81	44	33	-28	27		
IfStatement	-60	54							
import	95	88	-87	84					
integer	-3	2							
letter	1	1							
LoopStatement	-70	55							
ModuleDeclaration	-83	78							

MulOperator	49	-18	17						
number	50	19	-2						
octalDigit	-9	8	3	3					
PointerType	-40	25							
priority	95	-85	84						
ProcedureCall	-58	53							
ProcedureDeclaration	78	-72							
ProcedureHeading	93	-73	72						
ProcedureType	-41	25							
ProgramModule	97	-94							
qualident	82	80	45	43	34	26	21	19	-11
real	-5	2							
RecordType	-31	24							
relation	47	-14	13						
RepeatStatement	-67	55							
ScaleFactor	-6	5							
set	50	-21	19						
SetType	-39	24							
SimpleConstExpr	-15	13	13						
SimpleExpression	-48	47	47						
SimpleType	39	30	30	-26	24				
statement	59	59	-53						
StatementSequence	74	71	70	69	67	66	65	64	62
	61	60	-59						
string	50	19	-10						
SubrangeType	-29	26							
term	-49	48	48						
type	91	44	40	33	30	-24	23		
TypeDeclaration	76	-23							
VariableDeclaration	92	77	-44						
variant	-36	34	34						
WhileStatement	-66	54							
WithStatement	-71	56							

Appendix 2

The ASCII Character Set

	0	20	40	60	100	120	140	160
0	nul	dle		0	@	P	‘	p
1	soh	dc1	!	1	A	Q	a	q
2	stx	dc2	"	2	B	R	b	r
3	etx	dc3	#	3	C	S	c	s
4	eot	dc4	$	4	D	T	d	t
5	enq	nak	%	5	E	U	e	u
6	ack	syn	&	6	F	V	f	v
7	bel	etb	’	7	G	W	g	w
10	bs	can	(	8	H	X	h	x
11	ht	em	)	9	I	Y	i	y
12	lf	sub	*	:	J	Z	j	z
13	vt	esc	+	;	K	[	k	{
14	ff	fs	,	<	L	\	l	|
15	cr	gs	-	=	M	]	m	}
16	so	rs	.	>	N	↑	n	~
17	si	us	/	?	O	←	o	del

Layout characters

bs	backspace
ht	horizontal tabulator
lf	line feed
vt	vertical tabulator
ff	form feed
cr	carriage return

Separator characters

fs	file separator
gs	group separator
rs	record separator
us	unit separator

Index

K. Jensen, N. E. Wirth

PASCAL

User Manual and Report

Springer Study Edition
2nd corrected reprint of the 2nd edition. 1978.
VIII, 167 pages. ISBN 3-540-90144-2

PASCAL is a programming language which has been developed with the idea of systematic programming in mind. It is particularly suited for structured programming and non-numerical applications and the teaching of programming. It is distinguished by its organization of data structures, a small number of basic concepts and efficient implementation. This volume contains a revised report and a user manual which is directed to those who have previously acquired some programming skill. Chapters 0 to 12 of the user manual define the language PASCAL and serve as a standard for both the implementor and the programmer. Chapters 13 and 14 document the implementation of PASCAL on the CDC 6000 machine. The report describes a revised language incorporating the results of considerable experience gained through the use, teaching, and implementation of the original language PASCAL. In particular, many of the changes, and also some additional restrictions, were adopted and imposed in the interest of program portability and machine independent definability. This new revised edition continues to provide a means of learning PASCAL without outside guidance. Numerous corrections have been made in this reprint.

Springer-Verlag
Berlin
Heidelberg
New York

D. Gries

The Science of Programming

1981. XIII, 366 pages. (Texts and Monographs in Computer Science). ISBN 3-540-90641-X

Contents: Why Use Logic? Why Prove Programs Correct? – Propositions and Predicates. – The Semantics of a Small Language. – The Development of Programs. – Appendices 1–4. – Answers to Exercises. – References. – Index.

This is the first text to discuss the theory and principles of computer programming on the basis of the idea that a proof of correctness and a program should be developed hand in hand. It is built around the method first proposed by Edsger W. Dijkstra in his monograph *The discipline of Programming* (1976), involving a "calculus for the derivation of programs". Directing his materials to the computer programmer with at least one year of experience, Gries presents explicit principles behind program development, and than leads the reader through programs using those principles. Propositions and predicate calculus are presented as a tool for the programmer, rather than simply an object of study. The reader should come away with a fresh outlook on programming theory and practice, and the assurance to develop correct programs effectively.

Springer-Verlag
Berlin
Heidelberg
New York